VIEWS
~ *from the* ~
BOUNDARY

VIEWS
~ *from the* ~
BOUNDARY

Brian Johnston's celebrity interviews
from the commentary box

Editor Peter Baxter

TEST MATCH SPECIAL

BBC BOOKS

Published by BBC Books,
a division of BBC Enterprises Limited,
Woodlands, 80 Wood Lane, London W12 0TT

First published 1990

Introductions © Brian Johnston 1990
Interviews © the interviewees

ISBN 0 563 36023 2

Cover illustration by Dennis Curran
Inside illustrations by Rodney Shackell
Set in 11/14pt Janson by
Ace Filmsetting Ltd, Frome, Somerset
Printed and bound in Great Britain by
Redwood Press Ltd, Melksham, Wiltshire
Cover printed by
Belmont Press Ltd, Northampton

Picture Credits
Page 6 Courtesy of Pauline Johnston;
51, 60, 79, 130 and 164 Universal Pictorial Press;
69 Camera Press; 98 Monitor Syndication.
All other photographs © BBC.

CONTENTS

INTRODUCTION

 ONE OF THE things which I most enjoy on *Test Match Special* is the twenty-minute interview spot every Saturday lunchtime.

We invite well-known personalities from all walks of life to come and chat about themselves – and of course about cricket. In fact the only qualification they need for an invitation is a love of the game. If a guest can or has played cricket then so much the better, but otherwise watching, reading, viewing or listening are equally valid reasons.

The close affinity of the arts with cricket inevitably means that many of our guests are actors, writers, musicians and singers. But as you will see from the list of guests we have also had footballers, politicians, a weather forecaster and a jockey amongst others. Alas, so far we have not been able to entertain an actress. We were too late to ask those two ardent cricket watchers Celia Johnson and Gladys Henson, but we are still hoping to persuade Dame Peggy Ashcroft to join us in the commentary box. She is, we understand, a regular listener to *Test Match*

Special even when on a film set or during rehearsals for a play.

It's important to emphasise that all the interviews – or chats as we prefer to call them – are live from the commentary box, and never (with one exception) recorded in advance. They are completely unrehearsed and unscripted. We invite our guest to spend the day with us in the box. We give them a glass of champagne beforehand, the sponsors lunch on a tray afterwards – and even a piece of chocolate cake for tea!

The whole idea started one day in 1980 when Peter Baxter happened to be listening to Radio 4 in his car. To his delight he heard an interview with Ben Travers, famous for his Aldwych farces and an inveterate cricket follower all over the world. He was then aged ninety-four, but his memory of past heroes and past matches was completely unimpaired. By some magic he seemed able to recall the details of matches which he had seen over eighty years before. In Peter's own words 'I felt that there were great treasures stored in his memory bank. What a great idea it would be if we could invite Ben and others like him to come and talk to us about their love of cricket.'

And so it came to pass, though Ben was not the first selected. That honour fell to the lovable Ted Moult. The first Test, in 1980, was at Trent Bridge and as he lived nearby in Derbyshire he was an obvious choice to open the innings. Farmer, humorist, Brain of Britain, quiz expert extraordinary, he got us off to a perfect start in his usual jovial way.

The second Test was at Lord's and the scene was set for Londoner, Ben Travers.

BRIAN JOHNSTON.

BEN TRAVERS

WE WERE A BIT wary of asking Ben to join us as he was an elderly man and our commentary box is right up on the top of the pavilion at Lord's, with seventy-nine steps and no lift. John Arlott had cursed those steps for years. But we need not have worried. We sent a car to collect him from his flat near Baker Street, and Peter Baxter went down to meet him at the back door of the pavilion. They arrived in the commentary box with Peter puffing more than Ben. Five flights of stairs seemed to have had not the slightest effect on him. He was as perky as ever, a small birdlike figure with twinkling eyes and a slightly hooked nose. We were commentating as he entered the box and Peter sat him in a corner with his champagne. He stayed there alert, watching the cricket, and seemed quite undaunted at the 'ordeal' to come. After the lunchtime summary and a five-minute news bulletin from Broadcasting House, our conversation began.

It was intended that John Arlott and Trevor Bailey should join in, but as it turned out both they and I were superfluous. It was just like turning on a tap, with the occasional 'prompt' question. We all sat there in admiration and amazement. Without any notes his memories flooded back, and he seemed to relive every detail of what he had seen. He had a picture of all the players in his mind, their appearance, character and style. He flowed on non-stop until we were interrupted by the restart of play. We had been so enthralled that we even pinched an extra five minutes and skipped the lunchtime cricket scores.

We all congratulated him on his virtuoso performance, but as he ate his lunch, he seemed quite unaware of the effect he had had on all of us, and of course the listeners too.

At about 2.30 pm he got up, bade everyone goodbye and with his usual courtesy and good manners thanked *us* for allowing him to be our guest. I went down the stairs with him and saw him into his taxi. As I waved him off I didn't think that was the last time I would ever see Ben – but it was.

However, I was privileged to edit a book of his which resulted entirely from this broadcast. Michael Brown and Roger Houghton of Elm Tree Books had heard the broadcast, and immediately commissioned him to put it all down on paper. This he did with his complete professionalism, and delivered the script typed by himself bang on time four months later. The book was to have been called *94 Not Out*. But sadly Ben died just before its publication and the title was hurriedly changed to *94 Declared*. On the day before he died he wrote to thank me for helping with the book and saying once again how much he had enjoyed his visit to the commentary box. He apologised for the very few inaccuracies which I had corrected, explaining that he had not had a single *Wisden* to help him. A truly remarkable and lovable man.

LORD'S, 21 JUNE 1980

BEN TRAVERS   Well the first Test Match I saw – I think it was the first first-class match I saw – was at the Oval in 1896. I was nine years old and my father took me. They were three day matches in those days, of course.

It started on a Thursday and it rained most of the first day. They didn't start until after tea and W.G. Grace and F.S. Jackson opened for England, followed by Ranjitsinhji, and it shows that crowds were still enthusiastic because I remember that when Ranji came in to bat they started singing. I think he only made 7, it was a very low scoring match.

(In fact he made 8. Ed.)

BRIAN JOHNSTON   What did W.G. make, do you remember?

BEN   *(without hesitation)* Caught Trott bowled Giffen for 24. And he was out first. Jackson played a very good knock, but England won eventually.

It was a bowler's wicket.

(England won by 66 runs, making 145 and 84 to Australia's 119 and 44. Ed.)

And then later I saw W.G. When he left Gloucester he started London County at the Crystal Palace – a sort of club of his own. He used to get all the first-class cricketers to come and play for him on their days off, against the counties and that sort of opposition. And there I saw him make a hundred, with Ranji at the other end making another hundred – a very fine partnership. And then I saw him at the Hastings Festival. Oh, and I saw W.G. in one of the only two matches in which he played with Jack Hobbs; or rather in which Jack Hobbs played with him. He used to take the London County team to the Oval right at the beginning of the season. It was Jack Hobbs' first appearance. He made 80-odd.

BRIAN   Ben, before we talk about Jack Hobbs and the others, what was W.G. like as a man?

BEN   Well, of course he was a great hulk of a chap. He was the great predominant figure of cricket in his time – more so than any other individual since. He had rather an odd stance in that he cocked his left toe up. He had his left heel on the ground and cocked his toe up, and he also awaited the ball, when the bowler was half-way through his run, with his bat off the ground. Some comments have been made in recent years about modern batsmen who have done that; Tony Greig, Dennis Amiss, Mike Brearley and Graham Gooch, but W.G. started it, or at least he did it in his day.

He was, I would think, a humorous chap. I don't think he was very sensible.

BRIAN   Did you hear him talk?

BEN   Yes. Like another very large man, G.K. Chesterton, he had a curiously falsetto voice coming out of so huge a frame. He was also incidentally, you know, a practising doctor. My mother was born and brought up in Clifton and W.G. Grace was their family doctor. None of them lived very long. Except one; and she was a nun, so he didn't get at her, but the others all died young.

BRIAN   Did you ever see him disagree with an umpire? He's got that reputation.

BEN   Disagree! When I saw him make his hundred he was caught at short leg by a pro. called Brockwell, a Surrey pro., off the bowling of Lockwood for 24 or so, and he made out that it was a bump ball and he went towards

Brockwell flourishing his bat over his head as though he was going to fell him. So of course the umpire stood there utterly intimidated, gave him not out, and he went on to make a hundred.

BRIAN   Well, that was W.G. – a wonderful character. And what about Jessop, would you like to tell me about that?

BEN   There can't be many people about now who saw Jessop's classic 104 at the Oval in 1902. Oh, it was a wonderful occasion.

That was a very interesting Test Match. The Australians had already won the Ashes and this was the last Test. There was an Australian bowler there called Saunders. He was a brisk left arm spinner. In the second innings England had to make 263 to win. The first four batsmen in the England side were A.C. McLaren, L.C.H. Palairet, J.T. Tyldesley and Tom Hayward, and Saunders got them all four out for respectively 2, 6, 0 and 7. F.S. Jackson then went in and stayed there. This was just about the luncheon interval on the last day with these four wickets all down to Saunders. Old Hugh Trumble was bowling at the other end. He'd had 8 wickets for 65 runs in the first innings, so he was a menace, and I remember sitting on the right of the pavilion and seeing some of the elderly members leaving the ground disgruntled. They couldn't bear to see England so humiliated. Well, Braund, who came in with Jackson after lunch, was immediately out, to Trumble, for 2 and in came G.L. Jessop.

Jackson put up a wonderful defensive performance – a most sensible innings. At the other end Jessop went absolutely crazy. This menace Saunders, who'd already dismissed all our star batsmen, Jessop hit him for four fours in the square leg to long on district. Hugh Trumble was bowling at the other end. Jessop hit him on to the awning in the pavilion. The ball came back. He hit him there again

next ball. And so he went on. The enthusiasm was tremendous.

England had utterly no chance of course. But hadn't they? This thing began to dawn – this faint hope with this man going crazy. And in those days the boater hat was the fashion. Everybody wore one and I remember when Jessop made his century staid citizens everywhere removed their boater hats and threw them like boomerangs into the air. Unlike boomerangs they didn't return to their owners; a severe loss in those days, it was a great sacrifice. They must have cost at least three shillings a time. Oh, it was a wonderful sight!

And of course the most thrilling thing was the finish, because when Jessop was out and Rhodes came in to join Hirst, they wanted 15 runs from the last wicket. And there was the most canny piece of bowling by old Hugh Trumble. They made the runs gradually until the scores were tied and Hugh Trumble from the Pavilion End – he'd bowled right through the innings – had a chap called Duff, a very good opening batsman, at deep long on to the right of the Pavilion in what became known later as 'Sandham's Corner'. He served Wilfred Rhodes up a slow half-volley on the leg stump. Almost any batsman in the world would have said, 'Oh, here we are' – crack, wallop – hit it into the air and get caught by Duff. Not a bit of it. Wilfred Rhodes gently tapped it past square leg and ran the one run and that was that.

BRIAN You've made a lot of tours of Australia, haven't you?

BEN Yes, I've been there several times.

I was there, very luckily, in 1928/29 when I saw Bradman play his first innings for Australia against England in Brisbane. It was a great tour. Of course England had a wonderful side. Percy Chapman was captain and Jardine making his first tour and Farmer White; they were the three amateurs. Then there were Hobbs and Sutcliffe. I always say, Brian, that the greatest Test innings I ever saw was played by Jack Hobbs at Melbourne in the first few days of 1929, the Third Test Match, and he made 49. I think that 49 was the greatest innings I ever saw.

The wickets weren't covered in those days; they were at the mercy of the elements. They had a tremendous thunderstorm the night before and the sun came out the next morning and fairly baked the wicket, and the Australians still had two or three wickets to lose in their second innings. Farmer White polished them off in a couple of overs.

(Setting England 332 to win. Ed.)

Jack Hobbs said, 'I'm afraid we shall all be out by teatime.' And at teatime he and Sutcliffe were still there on what must have been the worst batting wicket anyone can conceive. I went and saw it at the close of play. It was like concrete with great lumps and holes in it – utterly terrible.

(For the record, England won by 3 wickets, and Sutcliffe made 135. Ed.)

BRIAN   What about the best batsman? Have you ever worked out the best batsman and the best bowler you've ever seen?

BEN   There are two kinds of batsmen, Brian, aren't there? There is the batsman who says, 'I'm going to slaughter you', and the batsman who says, 'You can't get me out.' I think the greatest 'slaughterer' I ever saw was undoubtedly Don Bradman. The greatest 'you-can't-get-me-outer' was Jack Hobbs and of course there were others like that. It's the approach to the game, not merely the execution; the mental approach to the game.

I think the 'can't-get-me-outers' could play fast innings if the circumstances arose, but it's the sort of general attitude to it: Hutton, Woodfull, Lawry, Boycott.

And then, of course, of the 'slaughterers' there are many. Well, we saw one yesterday.

(The previous day Viv Richards had scored a magnificent 145 in his first Test at Lord's, reaching his century in 125 balls and scoring 106 of his runs in boundaries. Ed.)

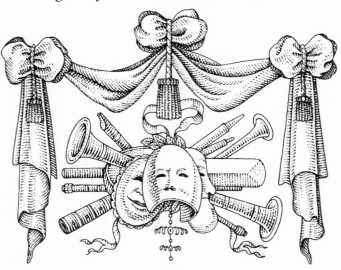

It's hard to believe, watching that innings yesterday, that there could ever be a better 'slaughterer' in cricket, but I think Don Bradman must be the tops.

BRIAN Did you see Trumper?

BEN Oh, yes.

BRIAN How great was he?

BEN He was great. But he wasn't all that graceful. He was supposed to be, but he wasn't. He had the most extraordinary stance, with his right knee bent in front of him. He was terrific. When I saw Bradman play at Melbourne in 1928, he made a glorious cover drive, and an excited member in the stand jumped up and said, 'Trumper!' and he was damn nearly lynched. It was blasphemy.

BRIAN Did you think then that Bradman was going to be a great player?

BEN Well, yes. We'd been told before the tour that there were two chaps who were up and coming cricketers. Archie Jackson and Don Bradman. Of course poor Archie Jackson would have been, I think, but he had consumption and died young. But, oh, Bradman, yes, he was terrific.

BRIAN Do you like watching wicket keepers?

BEN I think Alan Knott is tremendous. In my young days Bertie Oldfield was always supposed to be the best, and then he was superseded by Evans, and now by Alan Knott. But there was a very strange wicket keeper, a marvellous wicket keeper in my younger days who's still going strong, although not still keeping wicket, called Howard Levett. He used to stand up to fast bowling. Of course he couldn't do it today, unless he wore a pair of stilts, but that would rather handicap his wicket keeping I should think. He was an amazing chap.

BRIAN Just one more question, Ben, if we can. You wrote one farce about cricket called *A Bit of a Test*.

BEN   *A Bit of a Test*, yes. It wasn't expected to appeal to a very large public. It was after Douglas Jardine's tour with Larwood – the Bodyline row – and it was a sort of skit on that.

BRIAN   What was Ralph Lynn – captain of England?

BEN   No, I'm afraid Robertson Hare was.

BRIAN   Oh, purgatory and pandemonium!

BEN   He went in first with Ralph.

BRIAN   And Tom Walls, what was he – the villain?

BEN   No, Tom Walls merely produced. I think he kept out of it. I used to have great fun with Robertson Glasgow, dear old Crusoe. I remember picking a team from world history of those you would like to see playing in a Test Match. I had a wonderful opening pair: Beethoven and John the Baptist, with Attila the Hun as fast bowler, and Torquemada as the spinner. And marvellous umpires: Judge Jeffreys and Pontius Pilate.

BRIAN   On that note we've got to stop. We've had a marvellous twenty-five minutes and if it's ever raining at a Test here, may we ring you up to come and entertain us?

JOHN ALDERTON

HUMBERSIDE – AS it is now called – must have some secret ingredient in its air. It has produced three light comedy actors who live and breathe cricket. Brian Rix, Ian Carmichael – and our guest at the third Test in 1981 – John Alderton. He had come up especially from his old home town of Hull, the day after witnessing the Queen open the Humber Bridge.

Alders bears a remarkable likeness to Graham Gooch. It's uncanny. The only real difference between them is their cricket ability, though to be fair Alders is a good all-round club cricketer, and much in demand by the Lord's Taverners.

During our conversation he mentions the Primary Club. For those who don't know, this is a club which you are qualified to join if you have ever been out first ball in any class of cricket. There's an attractive club tie, and all money raised helps blind boys and girls to play games – especially cricket – or to take part in sports which, believe it or not, include skiing, golf and running. Every Saturday of a Test Match we remind listeners about the club, and tell them what to do to become members.

You may find our conversation a bit pessimistic about English cricket. But please remember that it took place on the third day of the most remarkable Test that I have ever seen. In a match interrupted by weather England followed on 227 runs behind, and at one point in their second innings were 135 for 7, still 92 runs behind. But thanks to a brilliant 149 not out by Botham, and some devastating fast bowling by Willis (8 for 43) England finally won by 18 runs. So had Alders and I been talking on that final Tuesday instead of the Saturday, our conversation would certainly have been more cheerful.

I started by telling him that I had always looked upon him as a Yorkshireman.

HEADINGLEY, 18 JULY 1981

JOHN ALDERTON   It's only just recently that I've started admitting that I wasn't actually born in Yorkshire, because F.S. Trueman has never let me forget it since he found out. The bombs were dropping in Hull in 1940 and all the women were taken into Lincolnshire, and when I was ten years old I found out that I couldn't play for Yorkshire. It took me an awful long time to get over that.
BRIAN JOHNSTON   But you're in good company – Lord Hawke, for example. Your mother wasn't trying to reach the border on horseback, like Lord Hawke's, was she?
JOHN   No, I think it was a charabanc.

BRIAN On your way up here all the small boys said, 'Please, Mr Gooch, can I have your autograph?' This has happened to you, hasn't it?

JOHN Yes, many times. I've signed his autograph so many times at Lord's, and been congratulated on many innings for which I've modestly accepted the praise. It all started in a Lord's Taverners' match, the first day Graham was picked for England, and I was playing with Bill Edrich. As we were changing he said, 'Congratulations. But I'm surprised to see you here today.' And I said, 'I like to turn out.' And after the fielding he was still quite convinced I was Graham Gooch.

It was only when I batted that doubts began to rise in his mind and he realised his mistake. But for the whole day he thought I was Graham Gooch, and ever since then when I've been stopped I've never denied it. It's quite a compliment.

BRIAN When did you start playing cricket? Like every Yorkshire boy, did you have a ball in your hand aged about two?

JOHN No, I didn't. My father didn't play cricket. I suppose I first got interested in cricket at about eight or nine. That's why I'm not pushing my son now. But of course then I used to go along to Anlaby Road in Hull and watch the great Yorkshire team of those days, always taking my sand shoes along in case they were going to be one short. And later, of course, I became known on television, and privileged to go into the Yorkshire dressing-room. It was a great thrill for me to be accepted in there, and to be privy to all the chat that goes on.

BRIAN We're not modest on this programme, so how good a cricketer are you?

JOHN I play pretty well from the commentary box. I've never played the kind of cricket in which one is allowed to become a member of the Primary Club, let's put it that way. They always give you one off the mark. I like tonking the ball. I've got a fairly good eye. I bowl a bit – although the arm's getting a bit lower now. I just love the game and if I had another choice in life and I couldn't become an actor I would love to be out there all day every day playing cricket.

BRIAN   There is this extraordinary business of the links between actors and cricket.

JOHN   It's gone on for as long as I can remember. In fact I was reading an article in *Strand* magazine, and the charity cricket and benefit cricket went on even then. Dan Leno turned out in full dame costume to play charity cricket. There's a photograph of it.

BRIAN   I would love to have seen that.

JOHN   There's always been a relationship between actors and cricketers. They seem to talk the same language. They enjoy each other's company and they have mutual admiration.

BRIAN   So did you always come to Yorkshire grounds to watch cricket?

JOHN   Yes, I did. In fact the first time I appeared on television was on this ground when the Australians were here in 1953. I ran on the field. But even before then I was interested in football. Do you remember Raich Carter, who was the player manager for Hull City? I was in a car park once, near the ground, having my orange juice and crisps and there was the great man standing there. I got out of the car and just stood in front of him. I didn't have the nous to ask for an autograph. I was far too shy for that. But he looked down at me and he said, 'Now then, son, do you want to be a footballer?'

I said, 'Yeah.'

He said, 'Do you want me autograph?'

I said, 'Yeah, yeah.'

I took it back to school and I was the king. And ever since then I knew what that autograph meant to me as a kid and I've never ever refused an autograph.

But, two years ago I was back at Hull City with my eight-year-old son. We were in the Directors' box, and at half-time we were having a drink and I suddenly spotted Raich Carter across the room. And I said to my son, 'In a minute, Nick. I'm going to take you across to meet one of the greatest footballers I've ever met. Finish your orange juice first.' I was a bit nervous about taking my son over to meet him and I wanted a quick word with Raich in preparation. Before I got there, there was a tap on my shoulder and Raich Carter had come across to me and said, 'Excuse me, Mr Alderton, I hope you don't mind me interrupting. Could I have your autograph for my son?'

And I said, 'Have I got a story to tell you.'

BRIAN   I used to collect autographs as a boy and I was refused once by Maurice Leyland, who was the nicest man there's ever been, at Taunton.

JOHN   It's a terrible shock, isn't it?

BRIAN   Well, it is. He and Waddington were walking across to a tent for lunch and it was obviously a bad time, and he said, 'Very sorry,' or something. You turn away and the tears well up in your eyes. If anyone asks me for an autograph I try like mad, unless I'm running to catch a train or something.

But in your visits to the dressing-room, who have been the great characters you've enjoyed most?

JOHN   Well, I just enjoy being part of it. And in the Yorkshire dressing-room, even when the times are hard and Boycs is out, the atmosphere is something to drink in and enjoy.

BRIAN   How long do you allow after Boycs has got out

before you go up and talk to him?

JOHN   I try and get out before he gets to the dressing-room.

BRIAN   He does feel it a bit, doesn't he?

JOHN   A touch, yes.

BRIAN   You leave him for an hour or two and then he's perfectly all right.

JOHN   You boys up here do a tremendous job, and wherever I go in the world I listen to your commentary. But, when you work it out, and I have once put a stopwatch on it, the time the ball is actually in play – and by 'in play' I mean from the time it leaves the bowler's hand to the time it hits the wicket keeper's gloves or it goes across the boundary – on the stopwatch, it works out at about eight seconds an over. Now, if you add that up during the day that's about twelve minutes' play. And you talk for six hours and make it sound absolutely tremendous!

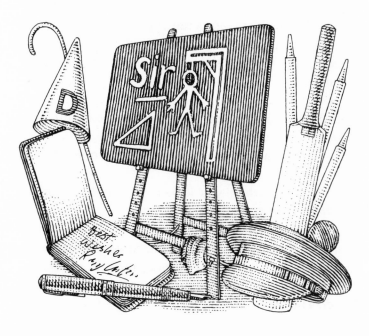

BRIAN   That's a very interesting statistic. I've never heard it. I've heard it as regards rugby football, where again there is very little actual play.

Your wife, Pauline (Collins), does she come to the cricket?

JOHN   No. We work together, sleep together and raise children together, and I think that's enough.

BRIAN   But she allows you your cricket.

JOHN   Oh, yes.

BRIAN   And does your management allow you to play cricket, or are you very heavily insured? I mean if you're injured when you're in a play it could be very awkward.

JOHN   Oh, I don't mind. I had my nose broken playing when I was eight.

BRIAN   How did you get it back in shape?

JOHN   It heals when you're young.

BRIAN   Have you a favourite amongst the roles you've played?

JOHN   Maybe *Please, Sir* because it was my first big break into situation comedy. But I enjoy it all. I enjoy every role I play. I usually enjoy the one I'm doing at the moment, whatever it is. I look forward to it. It's full of joy for me.

BRIAN   I've seen you being a rather nasty villain, and a sly sort of chap. You weren't very nice as the chauffeur in *Upstairs Downstairs*.

JOHN   Well, the Devil always plays the best tunes, doesn't he?

BRIAN   But which do you actually prefer. The laughs are the things, aren't they, really?

JOHN   I enjoy comedy, but you see for me comedy is easy. For other people it's very difficult. Although there is no greater thrill in the world than going into a theatre with an audience of two thousand people who don't know each other. They're all there in twos and threes, it's a cold day, the economy is bad and inflation's high, and after two hours they're together and they're rocking in their seats. To be lucky enough to have the ability to do that is something that I cherish. But it's something that you're born with, and I take very little credit for it. But I do get enormous enjoyment from playing baddies.

BRIAN But coming back to cricket, a cricketer's job is really to entertain, and recently there has been remarkably little entertainment for the average spectator.

JOHN I wonder how long the crowds are going to stand for it, because in the end it is the crowds that are paying for the cricket. The five-day Test Match may have changed in our minds because in the last five years we have got used to the one-day game and all the excitement that goes with it. But I see no reason why a game that lasts five days – and there is no other game in the world that lasts so long – should finish in a draw. What I would like to suggest to the TCCB and the players is that what we start thinking about is limited-over Test Matches, so there has to be a winner. We should have 125 overs each for the first innings, and a hundred for the second, and whoever gets the most runs wins.

BRIAN That would shock a lot of people, but I think it is a very good idea. Eton and Harrow have played a two-day match for goodness knows how many years. And they've had draw after draw after draw. The last two-day game was played this year, and next year they're going to start one-day matches. So, at last, they'll have to have a result. I think there's something in that. I wouldn't restrict it necessarily to 125 overs; I'd make it a bit longer than that, but limit the number of overs – I'd go along with that. It does come down to entertainment. Your job on the stage or the telly is to entertain, isn't it?

JOHN Yes, if I don't entertain, I don't get the job.

BRIAN With all these complaints about pitches, do you ever say, 'This is a rotten stage, I can't act'?

JOHN Acoustics really and sight lines are the only things that might bother me. But if you can play cricket, you can play cricket. It's the same for everybody. When you think back to a hundred years ago when they used to play on cow patches, and there was no lawn mower, and fielding was a bit of a lottery, scores were still being made and cricket was still entertaining. I don't see that because you've got a billiard table to play on that cricket can't be entertaining.

HENRY KELLY

THE WIDEST GRIN and the broadest accent on television. That's Henry Kelly. And, fairly rare for an Irishman, a wildly enthusiastic cricketer as a player, watcher and supporter. He's a great man for quiz shows either as presenter or contestant. He can also keep his end up in conversation in any company, his speed of delivery being slightly quicker than his bowling, which can best be described as medium and reasonably straight. He is one of those stars from the media who plays cricket for the Lord's Taverners, so helping to make large sums of money for various charities. It is surprising how well the mix of stars from the media and first-class cricketers seems to work, and the Lord's Taverners continue to draw large crowds wherever they play. Incidentally, Henry assures me that he was not the Irishman who was playing in a match which was being televised. He caught a brilliant catch at second slip, but then missed it on the action replay! I was interested to discover something of his early cricket background.

EDGBASTON, 31 JULY 1982

HENRY KELLY   I always say, Brian – and it's true – I only carry around one photograph of myself. It's tucked into my press card and it's me at the age of three in the front garden of our house in Athlone, County West Meath, which is right in the middle of rural Ireland, and I have a grip on the bat which I haven't improved. I've seen a lot of people play cricket at a very high level whose grip isn't as good and I haven't managed to do better than that since. My father and my brother were tremendous cricket enthusiasts and that's where I got my love for the game. It might sound corny, but I agree with the great socialist and cricket authority C.L.R. James who saw cricket as a microcosm of life if you like. I think it's unbeatable.

When we moved to Dublin from the country in 1953 we then had, for the next fifteen years, a wicket in the back garden which wasn't all that bad, and it was imperative that one didn't go to school in the morning without bowling at least half a dozen overs. Then in the evening I played cricket in the dark.

BRIAN JOHNSTON   How much cricket did you play then as a boy and what sort of club cricket was there?

HENRY   Despite all the other various and unfortunate divisions, cricket in Ireland is a one-state sport like rugby, which is terrific, and all the guys both north and south play on the same international side. Cricket in Ireland is about Minor County standard, let's not fool ourselves, and we're allowed now to play in the NatWest though not in the Benson and Hedges, and I think if we got some-where – I'd better be careful here at Edgbaston and not say Warwickshire – if we got Glamorgan in Dublin on a wet day we might get through one year, but it's about that standard.

As for me, I perfected the art of bowling straight off-breaks, which is a very subtle art, because as you know, you don't have to make them turn, you just have to make them think they're turning. I got most of my wickets by changing the field just before bowling the ball. If I give you the list of people I was once coached by, you can stand up and be impressed. I wrote them down before I came in. Charlie Hallows the Lancashire opening bat in the twenties and thirties – left-handed – didn't play as many Tests as he should have done. Cec Pepper, the Australian; Vic Cannings from Hampshire . . .

BRIAN Coaching still at Eton.

HENRY Indeed, and the one at which we should all bend the knee, the late Sir Frank Worrell. My most vivid cricket memory is of sitting in a tin shed one afternoon at Belve-dere College – it was raining – and Frank Worrell, who was then vice-captain of the West Indies touring side in Eng-land, was speaking to eleven ten-year-olds. He put chalk on one side of a ball and left the other side free and threw it across the hut from boy to boy to show how you could swing it and put different grips on it to show where the fingers should go.

BRIAN That's a good way of doing it. He was magic wasn't he, Frank Worrell?

HENRY Oh, what a lovely man.

I went to a Jesuit school – Belvedere – me and James Joyce and Terry Wogan and Tony O'Reilly, and other such luminaries of our time, and all the priests were ter-rific. We had one master, Father Brannigan, and he wasn't all that worried about tremendous skill on the pitch, but he wouldn't have you stopping the ball with your foot. He had rules like, 'Never cut in May', and 'Never cut until you're fifty'. It took me years to understand that, I thought that it meant fifty years of age. And there was 'A hard ball into the covers is no run', and 'Never run on a misfield', and 'The side that holds its catches wins its matches'. It was wonderful.

BRIAN   Were the priests any good at cricket?

HENRY   There was one tremendous priest who was my Latin master – Father Raymond Loler – who had an extraordinary nasal habit of saying 'nng' at the end of everything. He would say, 'H. Kelly will now bowl from the far endnng'. But he was a good batsman and a smashing slip fielder.

Cricket in Ireland, though, is always synonymous with the name of Jimmy Boucher. He was compared once with Clay and Tom Goddard in the thirties, and lots of touring sides – India, New Zealand and later on Australia – went back and said that there was this guy who was bowling fast off-breaks in a place called Ireland and he was terrific. He headed the first-class averages three times; in the thirties twice and again in 1948, because in those days Ireland played a lot more matches against county sides.

But in talking of Irish cricket we musn't forget 1969 when we got the West Indies out for 25, at a place called Syon Mills in County Derry, and it was so spectacular because the West Indies had lately come from doing a certain amount of damage to the then England team, but by about twenty minutes to one on that day the entire West Indian side was bowled out for 25. Dougie Goodwin took 6 wickets. It was the lead item on *The World at One*, in the days of the late Bill Hardcastle.

BRIAN   The pitch wasn't especially prepared in any way

to suit the Irish bowlers?

HENRY   No, because it's impossible to prepare a pitch to suit bowlers of third degree.

BRIAN   What was the name of the left arm over the wicket chap who captained them?

HENRY   Alex O'Riordan – an absolutely beautiful cricketer. He, too, was from my old school and he had the distinction of scoring a hundred at Lord's against the MCC. There are a lot of people who would unquestionably have made county sides.

BRIAN   How long have you been with us? I mean it's very nice . . .

HENRY   I came to live here in 1976, but funnily enough this year is the twenty-second anniversary of my first arrival as a schoolboy in England. I went to my first Test match at the Oval in 1960. It was the second last time that South Africa toured. Now in that match there was a man from Lancashire bowling tweakers, Tommy Greenhough. And he bowled for about three quarters of an hour against Jackie McGlew and there was hardly a run scored, it was really tense. And if I have any objection to the way

cricket has been modernised it is that in the television highlights in the evening we see the wickets and all the wonderful shots but not these tense periods which I find so fascinating.

We continued to make pilgrimages from 1960 until the early seventies.

BRIAN There's a big crowd that comes over now, you know, for the one-day matches and the Test Matches at Lord's.

HENRY We used to come over independently, though. A summer was not a summer to me unless I got the Yorkshire v Middlesex match . . . in which I first laid eyes on F.S. Trueman in the flesh.

BRIAN That's been a shock to a great many people.

HENRY I saw him bat once, and a finer player of a cover drive which completely fools fine leg, I haven't seen for years.

BRIAN Which county do you support?

HENRY I hope you will stand up when I say the team of Middlesex, of course. I have done since 1948. I think it was the first word I could say, and I think it was because of my brother. My father always looked at it as a game which ought to be supported rather than teams which ought to be supported. My brother was much addicted to one D.C.S. Compton and I think I followed on that one.

I heard you guys talking on the other channel, Radio 4, on *Tuesday Call* and this little boy phoned in and asked if he'd be able to hear the ball-by-ball from Australia during the winter. Well, that's part of my childhood, too. Crashing through the door at half-past six in the morning.

BRIAN I think it's rather lost something of its appeal now, because it's so clear you can hear every word. It was exciting when it surged back and forth and you used to strain to hear it.

HENRY   I used to think that was the noise of the crowd. It was only when someone explained to me that I realised it was atmospherics.

BRIAN   I don't know if you rule your wife properly. With mine I always have to have the radio under the pillow and keep it very quiet.

Have you ever done commentary?

HENRY   I have never. I've always thought I ought to be doing it, needless to say. It's the thing I would like to do most. We used to do mock ones when television first came. First we would turn down the sound and keep on the Third Programme, as it was then. And those were the days of Jim Swanton and Norman Yardley and I always thought there was a slight hint of teasing going on. Then we would try to do our own commentary but everybody would try to imitate Arlott's voice. I sound like John O'Arlott.

BRIAN   Tell us about this ridiculous programme *Game for a Laugh*, which was very funny. Tell us some of the things you made people do.

HENRY   We never made any extravagant claims for the programme. We said that there was nothing really intrinsically original in it. Lots of people would say, 'It's a bit like *Candid Camera*.' It's like a programme in the United States called *Games People Play*. There are a lot of people round this country who are doing things – maybe doing them for charity – they may be rolling a pea up a hill with their nose . . .

BRIAN   I'm doing that one.

HENRY   . . . And they only ever got on local television or local radio because there wasn't an outlet for that. Nor was there an outlet for a studio game which didn't have a huge prize. And there wasn't an outlet, Brian, for the type of thing that you did on *In Town Tonight*, when you tried, live on the wireless, to ride bareback on a circus horse. It was one of the funniest things I've ever heard in my life.

You also, if I'm not mistaken, lay down with an old-fashioned microphone strapped to your chest and let a train pass over you.

BRIAN   That's right. And someone washed his hands as he went overhead – at least I hope that's what he did.

HENRY   And did you not go into a post box at Christmas and when they put letters in a voice said, 'Oi, you've put the wrong address on.'?

BRIAN   And I put my hand out to take a letter and a lady fainted when she saw the hand come out.

HENRY   Now that is fun. So we decided to combine all those elements and have a studio game with a few, in the corny phrase 'ordinary people', doing extraordinary things, and it just mercifully seemed to take off.

We once put a ladder up outside Barkers in Kensington on Friday the thirteenth. The object of the exercise was to find out whether people were superstitious or not. At first we thought the answers were unbroadcastable – not because of any vulgarity or obscenity – but because the story didn't work. When we looked at the film we found that it was because people didn't do the things we expected them to. I said to one guy, 'Excuse me, please, I saw that you avoided walking under that ladder. Are you superstitious?' And he said, 'Nah, mate. I saw you were filming and I didn't want to get in the way.'

And there was another lady who came up and I said, 'I saw you avoided the ladder. Are you superstitious?' And she said, 'Absolutely not.' So I said, 'Did you know today's Friday the thirteenth?' She said, 'Oh really? How very interesting.' I said, 'You're not superstitious; is your husband superstitious?' 'I'm not married.' 'Any of your family superstitious?' I'm on my last legs by now; didn't know what to say to this lady next. And then she suddenly looked me up and down and she said, 'You've kissed the Blarney, young man. Ha ha ha ha!' and went off. And we were able to incorporate that in the end because the joke turned back on me and I was made to look if not a complete fool, at least sufficiently foolish to make an item.

BRIAN   Is there an Irish cricket story?

HENRY   The sun is now shining at Edgbaston and we encourage all the people to come along and watch the cricket, so therefore you haven't time to hear all the Irish cricket stories.

My best is one which involved me. It should really have been referred to Lord's. I was at the non-striking end when the ball was delivered to the batsman at the other end, who played it hard into the covers. Rule number one: a hard ball into the covers – no run. So, although it wasn't my call, as he still had his head down, I said, 'No.' I'd advanced about four yards down the pitch *à la* Randall, because I was a bit of a fidget, and I turned and walked back to the crease. In the meantime the ball was returned to the wicket keeper, who promptly took off the bails and appealed, and the square leg umpire's finger went up. I was brought up never to challenge the ruling of an umpire, but I did say to the umpire at my end, 'Who's out? I can't be out, because I'm at the wrong end.' And the batsman at the wicket keeper's end said, 'I can't be out, because I never left my ground.'

The umpire came back and said, 'We don't know, but one of youse is out.' And one of us had to go, and as it was an old friend of mine, who was an aspirant priest batting at the other end, who was obviously much better than me, I naturally sacrificed my wicket and walked away.

BRIAN   A charming story, which reveals the very best of you and the very best of cricket.

MICHAEL BENTINE

IF EVER I AM FEEL-ing low, which luckily is very seldom, I have one immediate and certain cure. I put on the tape of my interview with Michael Bentine at the Lord's Test in 1983. I defy anyone who listens to it not to laugh – in my case hysterically. The good news is that the transcript of the interview also comes over as a very funny piece. We miss of course his high-pitched voice usually accompanied by a giggle, and his amazing range of accents and voices. Perhaps my favourite was his imitation of Howard Marshall recording a commentary on D-Day from a shell-hole on the Normandy beaches.

Benters, as I call him, is a most unlikely old Etonian, as he enjoys nothing more than taking the mickey out of the establishment. For those who don't know, at Eton we used to call someone who played cricket a 'dry bob', and a rowing man a 'wet bob'. Oh yes, and a 'chinaman' to which Benters refers is the left-hand bowler's off-break, which he claims he was able to bowl. And a 'sixpenny' was the first cricket colour you could get at Eton.

Apart from all his joking, leg-pulling and comedy routines, underneath it all Benters is a very serious person. He is an expert on nuclear matters and a believer in the supernatural and extra-sensory perception. He can, and does, talk seriously about these matters, but often when you least expect it, there is a change of voice and out comes some outrageous joke or piece of mimicry. He is a great entertainer who unfortunately these days is seldom seen or heard. But we were lucky to get him on *Test Match Special*.

LORD'S, 13 AUGUST 1983

BRIAN JOHNSTON   When you were at Eton, were you a dry bob or a wet bob?

MICHAEL BENTINE   I was a dry bob, very much so. In fact, when I was arrested for desertion . . . which was interesting, because I wasn't in the RAF at the time. There was a very slight screw-up over the names and I was still waiting to go into the RAF, because I volunteered many times, but they kept on saying things like, 'But you're of non-European descent'. And I said, 'Well, even in this light I can almost pass for white.' Because in those days they were the most discriminating lot you've ever met in your life. And eventually this chap turned up with the RAF police uniform at the Westminster, where I was working, and he said, 'Mr Michael Bentine?'

So I said, 'Yes,' thinking, 'At last. They've accepted me. I'm in.'

And he said, 'You're a deserter. Sixty-five days adrift.'
And I found myself here at Lord's in front of A.H.H.
Gilligan, the captain of England, who was, of course, prac-
tically God, and he said, 'You can't be a deserter, you're an
Etonian.' I said, 'I'm not only an Etonian, but I'm a Peru-
vian; the only Peruvian ever born in Watford – and
they've arrested me and I haven't been in the RAF yet.'
And he said, 'I know, there's been the most terrible muck-
up about the whole thing.' And then he said, 'When you
were at Eton were you a dry bob or a wet bob?' And I said,
'I was a dry bob, sir.' 'Get your sixpenny?', 'Yes, sir,' I said.
'Play for your house?' 'Yes, sir.' 'Not a bowler, are you?'
'Yes, sir. Slow left arm.' 'Can't bowl a chinaman, can you?'
I said, 'Yes, I can bowl the chinaman.' He said, 'Must have
you in the RAF.' I could have been Hitler's adopted son,
so long as I could bowl the chinaman.

BRIAN   You know you're talking about the chairman of
selectors, Peter May's late father-in-law.

MICHAEL   Really? There were two Gilligans, weren't
there?

BRIAN   Yes, A.E.R. was Arthur, and this was Harold.
So what were you, a bowler, a batter or both?

MICHAEL   I was an appalling batsman, because I suppose
my eyes were beginning to go, and by 1943 I think I was
the only aircrew cadet who needed a braille instrument
panel. But when they caught me trying to get the guide-
dog into the front turret, there was murder. They put me
into Intelligence which shows how desperate we were in
1943. And that all happened here at Lord's.

And those were the days of Howard Marshall, with that
lovely voice, 'A beautiful day here, with the tracery of
clouds – a perfect setting.' He never told you about the
cricket, but he told you everything else about the game.
And the next time I saw him was on the beach-head in

Normandy.

BRIAN   What were you doing there – Intelligence?

MICHAEL   Theoretically, but at the time I was praying. Unfortunately my truck had sunk. They'd opened the doors of the landing craft and I'd said, 'Forward!' and it went into about eighty feet of water and we sort of floated ashore with these life-jacket things on and I spent about three days trying to find my unit, saying, 'Excuse me, old chap . . .' 'Get down, you're drawing fire!' And this chap was in a shell hole and I heard this voice. He'd got this huge machine with him, which made recording discs and he said, 'It's a lovely day here on the beach-head and you can hear the sound of the shells going over and earlier – of course you couldn't see them, but you could hear them – the gliders whistling through the air.' And I thought, 'We can't possibly lose, because Howard Marshall's here.'

BRIAN   Now you speak how many languages?

MICHAEL   I don't really. Everybody thinks I'm a linguist. I stagger along in several. I spoke French and Spanish, so the British put me with the Poles instantly.

BRIAN   You've been a bit shocked today by the short pitched bowling.

MICHAEL   I was shattered by those bouncers coming in. 'Oh yes, he's hit him! Well done! Right on the side of the head! Fractured skull!' And they're all wearing crash helmets and body armour. It's like American Football.

BRIAN   What did you do when you played?

MICHAEL   Ducked a lot. No, I didn't even wear a box in those days – I wasn't all that well developed.

BRIAN   You were one of the original cast of *The Goon Show*. How many of those did you do?

MICHAEL   Oh, Lord knows, I did an awful lot. I was one of the original four and I always felt that four was too many. Three's a magic number; four's not really a magic number.

It was great fun doing it. I did it for about two years in the run up to it, and then I think I was with them for about two-and-a-half years, and I'm still with them in spirit.

BRIAN Is the humour of the Goons unique?

MICHAEL I think it's the most magnificent rubbish ever written. It's absolute nonsense. We used to get away with murder. We had 'Singes Thing', the Irish arsonist, at a time when there was still the influence of Reith, who was very Calvinistic.

BRIAN But you were censored a bit on the Goons, weren't you?

MICHAEL Well, they used to say things like, 'You can't say that, the inference is revolting,' and they didn't realise that we were using terrible tag-lines like, 'It's your turn next in the barrel.' But they hadn't been in the services and we were all ex-servicemen and we couldn't have cared less. They'd try and read into it all sorts of meanings, and they were all old Army jokes, old Navy jokes or old RAF jokes.

BRIAN Which voices were you?

MICHAEL I was the original Henry Crun, and I was Pure Heart who was one of these idiots with lines like, 'Start up the engines of the mighty Brabazon,' and you would hear the sound of a steam train pulling out of a station and he'd say, 'Ask the chief designer to step into my office.' It was all that insanity and people read into it as though it was some sort of intellectual exercise.

BRIAN Now, I didn't see you on the halls, but didn't you have an act with a bit of a chair? What did you do with it?

MICHAEL I was desperate. I moved a lot. With an act like mine, you've got to keep moving. I did have this back of a chair which I'd broken when I was with my brother and sister-in-law, and it had fallen off and it looked like a sub machine gun and my brother had picked it up and said, 'I'll shoot you with it.' And I thought, what a marvellous

idea, and I made things out of it and I did a lot of those things afterwards.

BRIAN Well, you did something with that thing you shove down a drain.

MICHAEL A sink plunger. Yes, that became the last trolley bus in England and all sorts of strange things – Long John Silver by shoving it on the knee – and I stuck it on my face, it nearly killed me, broke my nose, too.

BRIAN Do you like working by yourself, then?

MICHAEL Well, I've always been a loner essentially. I stammered so dreadfully until I was about sixteen, but at Eton a man called Burgess taught me to speak with 'a swing-and-a-rhythm-and-a-pause-and-a-run.' And the first thing I did was to walk into the Soc Shop, which of course is the tuck shop, and they all stopped as if I was the gun-fighter who'd just come through the double doors. And I walked in and declaimed, 'N-may I have n-fishcake.' And there was a dead silence and the lady said,

'What sort, dear? You want salmon or you want ordinary fish?' I went, 'Well er, er, er,' because I'd only learnt the first bit. And then I learnt to say 'N-bangers and n-mash.' So I lived off bangers and mash.

BRIAN How did you cure your stammer?

MICHAEL I slowly learnt the vocabulary. I got the food first and then I used to come into the shop to great choruses of, 'N-may he have n-fishcake.' Well, you know what a mad school it was.

BRIAN And then you had this TV series *It's a Square World.* This was your own thing, wasn't it?

MICHAEL Oh yes. I've always written my own stuff. It was a sort of conglomerate-type mad news programme which later became things like *Not the Nine O'Clock News* and *Monty Python* and generally got filthed up, whereas when I did it they were dead clean, but only because we weren't allowed to be anything else. I once got hauled up for burning a brick, because I used to destroy Television Centre in pretty well every programme. I used to burn it up or send it into space or destroy it with a *Gardening Club* giant man-eating orchid, and on this occasion I'd burnt a brick with a smoke machine. There was hell to pay. And they sent me this marvellous memo, which I have framed. It says, 'Under no circumstances must the BBC Television Centre be used for the purposes of entertainment.' One chap said to me, 'If it wasn't for you lot, this would be a good job.' I said, 'If it wasn't for us lot, you wouldn't have a job.'

42

RICHARD STILGOE
AND PETER SKELLERN

IN 1983 I WAS AN unsuspecting victim of Eamonn Andrews on *This is Your Life.* The Lord's Taverners turned up in force and among them was Richard Stilgoe – an old friend. At the reception afterwards he intimated to Peter Baxter that he would love to appear on *Views from the Boundary.* We were of course delighted, not only because we know he turned out for the Lord's Taverners, but because he is quite simply – to me at any rate – the best cabaret artist of the present day. He's a pianist, singer, lyricist, composer, teller of jokes and outrageous puns, and has the amazing ability to make an anagram from anybody's name. He has also given one-man shows, which led to a very successful partnership with pianist/singer Peter Skellern.

It was, therefore, not surprising that shortly before the Oval Test in 1983 Richard rang Peter Baxter and asked whether he could bring a friend with him. The friend was of course Peter Skellern and for the first – and only time so far – I conducted a dual conversation on the programme with these two gifted entertainers.

However, had all this happened in the summer of 1989 I would not have been quite so keen on Stilgoe. He and I appeared with Harry Secombe in one of his *Highway* programmes. It was recorded in April on the famous Broadhalfpenny Down cricket ground by the Bat and Ball Inn at Hambledon, the cradle and centre of cricket for thirty years or so from 1750. We were all dressed in blazers and white flannels, and the programme, which included at least four cricket items, was to be broadcast in the height of summer by ITV.

As luck would have it this particular day was the coldest in April for many years, and we sat freezing in deck-chairs pretending it was a gorgeous summer's day. There were dew-drops on our noses, and Harry – who because of his diabetes feels the cold more than most – was visibly shivering as he interviewed me. The ground is very exposed and there was a biting cold wind, and I couldn't resist saying to him, 'I reckon on a cold day it must be freezing playing cricket up here.'

One of the cricket items was a song about Hambledon especially composed for the occasion by Richard. There he was at a white piano in the outfield, blue with cold and trying to play with numb fingers. However, he managed nobly, and when I saw the programme in June you would never have guessed that it was not a hot, sunny summer's day.

I admired his skill as a pianist and singer, but I did take exception to one or two lines that took the mickey out of me and my old age. There were three choruses, and at the end of each there was a couplet. Here they are:

So it all began in Hambledon, a billion years ago
Brian Johnston saw it – and he ought to know.

Yes it all took place at Hambledon as the world began to wake

And Brian Johnston watched while eating prehistoric cake.

But it all began at Hambledon – it did – I do declare
Brian Johnston told me – and he knows 'cos he was there!

You see what I mean? But of course I've forgiven
Stillers.

THE OVAL, 27 AUGUST 1983

BRIAN JOHNSTON   Let's start with Skellers. Are you a
player of cricket or a watcher?
PETER SKELLERN   I'm a player. I'm really waiting for Bob
Taylor to get injured. I play village cricket now and I
played when I was at school. I was wicket keeper at
cricket, goalkeeper at football and full back at rugby,
which are all the 'hands' positions, and great for a pianist.
BRIAN   Looking at your hands . . . for such a pianist, those
are rather big mitts.
PETER   You do need them, you know. People believe
you're supposed to have long elegant fingers to play the
piano, but it's all wrong really. You need big meaty hands
to do it properly. But I can play all sorts of music, except
rock'n'roll, because it actually hurts my fingers to do that.
RICHARD STILGOE   This is in fact because he is protecting
his wicket keeping skills all the time. I play rock'n'roll
quite a lot because I'm a slow bowler and it strengthens
the spinning finger.
BRIAN   It's very brave of him actually, as a pianist, to keep
wicket because you can get the odd knock on the finger.

PETER Well, I broke my finger once.

BRIAN Did that affect your playing at all?

PETER Yes it did for a year. I couldn't stretch the octave and I had to re-learn to stretch, and it still aches after a couple of hours.

BRIAN Stillers, you play nowadays for the Taverners. Were you ever a very good player?

RICHARD No, I was appalling, I was absolutely dreadful.

PETER That's not what you said to me.

RICHARD It's very difficult, because, like everybody else who can't play cricket, I bowl slow leg-breaks, or I say they're slow leg-breaks and we just happen to be unlucky and they're not turning today. I am in fact the natural successor to Underwood but no batsman in the world knows this, so they hit me out of the ground.

BRIAN How would you describe your occupation? Are you an entertainer?

RICHARD Well, as partly an entertainer and partly a cricketer, I suppose 'a Tavaré artist' would be about the closest.

BRIAN But you write all your own material, and you're very good at producing a lyric at a moment's notice, about anything!

RICHARD Well, not at a moment's notice, if you're about to ask me to do one. It's my day off. I write songs about almost everything except cricket, because I'm terribly serious about cricket. I wouldn't dream of making jokes about it; it's far too important.

BRIAN But your other great skill is making anagrams of people's names.

RICHARD I'm jolly lucky in that my name happens to rearrange itself into a lot of useful other names, like Sir Eric Goldhat, who is the richest man in the world. Then there's Dr Gloria Ethics, who you will seldom meet, and my favourite other one is Giscard O'Hitler, who is president of the whole of Europe.

BRIAN   Can you do anyone from the commentary box?

RICHARD   You're a rather difficult lot. Your name, for instance, has got a 'J' in it. It's very hard to hide a 'J'. I did once, years and years ago, work with an American group called the Tin Horn Banjos . . . and if you rearrange them you get . . . Brian Johnston.

BRIAN   What about Sir Frederick Trueman, now? Is it possible to get one out of him?

RICHARD   Usually, when you rearrange the name, you get something completely different from the character of the person, which is why, if you rearrange 'Fred Trueman' you get 'ruder fat men', which is obviously nothing like the character itself.

The longer names are, of course, harder, I mean Christopher Martin-Jenkins – you get almost the whole of 'War and Peace' if you rearrange that.

BRIAN   How long does it take you to write what are very much up-to-date lyrics?

RICHARD   Like anybody in journalism, really, you do it at the last minute and you rely on the adrenalin to get it done. It is easier to write a speech twenty minutes before you've got to make it than it is four weeks before, because terror gets it written for you.

BRIAN   Skellers, when did you start this mixture, you in the white tie and tails, and then suddenly a brass band appears? It seems strange until you hear it and then it's an absolutely marvellous mixture.

PETER   I was in the National Youth Brass Band when I was a boy. I played trombone. Being brought up in a Lancashire mill town, bands were all round you and that was the music that was made. The first hit song I did was *You're a Lady* and it was about a northern girlfriend, so I decided to use a brass band rather than an orchestra. And it worked a treat. It surprised me too; it surprised everybody.

BRIAN   How long did that take you to write?

PETER   A morning – I sound like Ernie Wise – actually I wrote twelve songs in ten days all of which were among my better songs, and all were used. It was just some brainstorm that I had, and that was one of them.

BRIAN   Does that happen with you, Stillers?

RICHARD   Not always, but you do certainly get a week when you write some definitely second division stuff, rather than the fourth division stuff, and then four weeks when you can't write anything at all, however hard you try.

BRIAN   Do you keep bringing yourself up to date?

RICHARD   You change the name of the Prime Minister whenever it's necessary, yes. It's been very difficult, actually, for all male performers having a lady Prime Minister.

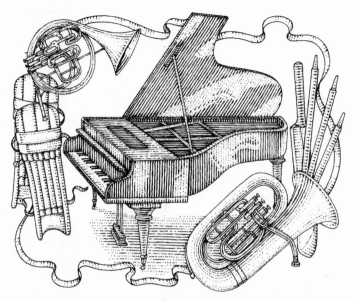

It brought Janet Brown to the fore and sent the rest of us rather into the background. I'm still working on my Neil Kinnock impression.

BRIAN Have you got the Welsh lilt?

RICHARD Oh no, it's mainly combing the hair across the top of the head that I'm working on.

BRIAN You wrote a song about Lillee and Thomson. Were you the first to think about 'Lillian Thomson' as a woman?

RICHARD I think I originally thought of 'Lillian Skinner', because of the shoe shop. She became 'Lillian Massie' in the year when Massie got all those wickets at Lord's, and then, when Thomson took over 'Lillian Thomson' started off, and I did this song which was then made hugely popular by Rachael Heyhoe, I think.

BRIAN Can you give us the words?

RICHARD It's all about slips and covers and things and it's quite improper. I'm not sure if I can remember the words; I'm not sure if I should. It's mainly that in Lillian

Thomson Australia have the world's best opening pair.
BRIAN   Oh, I see, it's that sort of song.
RICHARD   Which is why I'm not going to sing it for you now.
'She is the fastest lady bowler the world has ever seen.
Her bumper's awe-inspiring and her language far from clean.'
That is quite enough of that.

(At that point in the interview the quartet of Johnston, Stilgoe, Skellern and Martin-Jenkins were brave enough – some would say ill-advised enough – to launch into a fully (vocally) orchestrated version of The Way You Look Tonight, *which was relayed to the unfortuante spectators at the Oval who had previously been enjoying their lunch. Ed.)*

DEREK NIMMO

DEREK NIMMO caused quite a sensation as he walked through the long room at the Oval when he was our guest for the fifth Test in 1984. He might have come straight off the set of the play, *White Cargo* ('Oh the flies and the heat!').

He was wearing a white suit, panama hat, white shoes and a red carnation in his buttonhole. Round his neck was a pair of field-glasses, bedecked with badges from racecourses all round the world, including the famous Melbourne Cup which he attends every year. All he really lacked was a fly-whisk.

He must have one of the most recognisable voices in the whole world of entertainment. He has a languid rather upper class drawl, admirably suited to the many clerical roles he has played. The most famous of these was the curate called Noot in the highly popular tv series *All Gas and Gaiters*.

There is a story about Derek which I cannot resist telling, although he himself always indignantly denies it. He was playing one of the clergymen in that hilarious farce

See how they Run. Derek did not have to appear until the start of the second Act, so he used to dine at home and drive down to appear at the Shaftesbury Theatre in time to go on stage at about nine o'clock. Bill Pertwee was also in the cast and assures me that one night Derek – possibly having had too good a dinner – went to hide in a cupboard two pages of script *before* he was meant to. The result, as you might expect, was temporary chaos as the cast tried to adjust their lines to fit the new situation. But being true professionals they got out of it somehow.

Derek also excels in playing the typical silly ass Englishman, and often pretends to be one in real life. Though he is in fact a highly intelligent person and a very efficient and successful impresario, organising theatrical companies to tour the Far and Middle East, which remain extremely popular.

However, there is one thing that I regret I could not persuade Derek to do for us in the commentary box, perhaps just as well because it was a very hot day. He has double jointed toes and can wriggle and twiddle them as if he were playing the piano with his feet. He did this nightly for five years in the long-running musical *Charlie Girl.* At one time he was the presenter in a tv chat show and asked me to appear on it. At the end of the show he said he had heard that I could tuck my ears in (which I can), and asked me to demonstrate this to the audience. I said I would do so if he did his toe trick. So he took off his shoes and socks and we did a double act for the surprised audience.

Needless to say Derek is an ardent cricket follower and usually tries to combine his theatrical enterprises to coincide with the Test Matches in Australia.

THE OVAL, 11 AUGUST 1984

BRIAN JOHNSTON Nimmers, before I ask you anything else, the tie you're wearing, will you tell us what it is?

DEREK NIMMO It's not one that I would choose to wear at Lord's, but I thought I might just get away with it here. It is the Kerry Packer tie. It's a sort of bastardised MCC tie with a little bit of pale blue in between. I thought it might annoy you slightly, Johnners, so I thought I'd put it on.

BRIAN It's made me very angry indeed, because somebody once sent me a tie not saying what it was and I wore it at a county match here. It happened to be another Packer tie, which I didn't know, and I was shunned.

But on to you and your cricket. Born in Lancashire, so did you play cricket as a boy?

DEREK I played at school. I was never any good, but I've watched cricket from my earliest days, really, and I remember one of my more exciting moments during the Old Trafford Test against the Australians in 1948. I got Denis Compton's autograph and I got Bill Edrich's, but I didn't get Bradman's. I just couldn't get anywhere near him in the whole five days. Then, when I was at the Adelaide Test in 1979, I actually managed to get Bradman's autograph. It had taken me some thirty years, but I finally got it. I was sitting in the George Giffen stand there with Neil Harvey on my left hand side and Bradman on my right, and I watched England actually win the Fifth Test at Adelaide.

BRIAN Why do you think there is this great rapport between people on the stage like yourself and cricketers?

DEREK I think one of the things is that we generally work at night and therefore we're one of the few groups of people who can afford the luxury of attending a three-day game and of course a five-day Test match.

BRIAN And of course you're very lucky because you travel regularly every winter to climes where they play cricket.

DEREK Yes, I go increasingly to the Middle East, and it's rather exciting to watch cricket in Dubai, Abu Dhabi, Muscat, Bahrain, or wherever it might be. There are so many indentured workers coming in from the subcontinent, from Sri Lanka, India and Pakistan, who are good cricketers that out there in the middle of the sand they'll put down a matting pitch or they'll actually grow grass to play on. In Bahrain they've got grass pitches now. There's a tremendous interest in cricket and of course there are a lot of British ex-patriots over there, so you can see the growth of cricket in that part of the world.

BRIAN Who's been your particular hero? Did you have any Lancashire heroes? Have you always followed Lancashire?

DEREK Well, yes. All the Stathams and the Washbrooks, those sort of people, were my childhood heroes. But you see I wander round in a sort of dilatory way, so I don't attend permanently at Lord's or wherever it might be for the season, just wherever I find cricket I pop in and look at it.

I remember once getting a cable from you saying, 'Hello, Nimmers. Blowers and Johnners arriving' when I was in Australia.

BRIAN You were performing, I think, in Adelaide.

DEREK I was actually asked to do the first commentary

ever on commercial radio in Adelaide. It had always been the prerogative of the ABC. But there was a rather curious tie to it all, because we weren't actually allowed to describe the bowling. We were only allowed to 'commentate' between deliveries. So when anything was actually happening you had to talk about the pigeons flying over the cathedral and that sort of thing . . .

BRIAN Rather like we do.

DEREK . . . and then say, 'five runs were scored in that over.' So it did rather hold things up a bit. It wasn't a frightfully good idea. But at least we won that particular Test.

I was awakened eighteen months ago at half past three in the morning when Australia won the Adelaide Test, and a voice on the telephone said, 'Hello, Derek, you're live on air to Australia Radio 5 DN, just to say what do you think of it?' I said, 'What do I think of what?' I thought Hawke had been assassinated. Typical Australian; no regard for whether it was three or four in the morning.

But Australian hospitality is really quite alarming, I find. I remember once I was doing a play there for about four or five months, my liver was beginning to turn up a bit, and I thought I wanted a holiday. At first I thought I'd go up to the Barrier Reef and then I thought, 'I won't. I'll get out of Australia completely,' because we'd been overwhelmed with parties and hospitality. So my wife and I decided we'd go to Penang – 'the Pearl of the Orient'. And as we arrived in our tolerably small plane, behind us came a Qantas 747 and the banners were unfurled saying, 'Welcome, Adelaide–Penang Week' and off the plane came four hundred hearty Adelaidians, led by Don Dunstan, who was then the Premier, in natty pink shorts. And for the whole of my lovely escapist week in the Pearl of the Orient, we had boomerang throwing and Penfold wine drinking and wood chopping. And people would say to me, 'Ah, here's the mad monk.' They're very nice and charming really, aren't they?

BRIAN   And, of course, you love what they love – racing. You arrived today with about sixty racing badges, paddock entries and members things tied to your binoculars.

DEREK   Well, I do leave them on. My wife says it's extremely vulgar, but I try to get down to the Melbourne Cup, which is the great love of my life.

BRIAN   When you were performing in *Charlie Girl* you did this amazing thing of wiggling your toes. When did you discover you could wiggle your toes in that way? Are you genuinely double jointed?

DEREK   They're just deformed, basically. What happened was, I was doing a play in Johannesburg with the lovely Moira Lister, and we were lying in bed together – rehearsing, I hasten to say – and we couldn't think of an end to the first act.

BRIAN   I could suggest one.

DEREK   Well, that might have been too climactic, I think. Anyway, she suddenly looked at my feet and said, 'What very funny toes you've got.' I was very slightly offended, as you would be and so I said, 'Can I have a look at yours.' Then we got the stage hands to take off their shoes and socks, and it was decided by a fairly large majority that my toes were a bit odd. Then I put them into this play in Johannesburg, and the play didn't go frightfully well and I didn't get very good notices, but my toes had an absolute triumph. They took all the notices. Then I came back to do *Charlie Girl* with Dame Anna Neagle, and there was a scene which we couldn't quite get right and I suddenly remembered my toes. So we put them into that and again the show got awful notices, and I didn't take home any success, but my toes were noticed, you see.

BRIAN You do this amazing radio programme, which I have taken part in, *Just a Minute*. You're very good at it.

DEREK Well, you see, you have to talk rubbish. That's why I'm so good.

BRIAN If I were to say, 'Do a minute on, shall we say, a Botham bouncer,' could you just ad lib like that?

DEREK No.

BRIAN Have a shot.

DEREK No.

BRIAN You won't do it?

DEREK No.

BRIAN Do you think of them beforehand, then?

DEREK No. It's just that one gets an additional fee for doing *Just a Minute*, and it gets worldwide repeats. But I think Freud is the best and Kenneth Williams is very good. Freud goes very slowly. I went to his sixtieth birthday party at the House of Commons and there were a lot of very good speeches – Norman St John-Stevas, Jeremy Thorpe and people – and Freud said in his, 'I'd just like to say that all my dearest friends in the whole world are here today. You may also have noticed that there are now seventeen Liberal Members of Parliament, and you may perhaps have observed that I am the only Liberal Member of Parliament here tonight.'

BRIAN   I wonder what the other sixteen thought.

DEREK   And another time he won the right to one of those private member's bills. You know, they have a sort of raffle in the House of Commons. And I said to Freud, 'What are you going to bring in – proportional representation?' 'No,' he said, 'I don't think it's sufficiently emotive. I will couple proportional representation with the legalisation of bestiality and call it "One man one goat."'

BRIAN   Tell me why you have a penchant for clerical roles. You've done a lot of those on the telly.

DEREK   Well, I've got a rather pompous voice you see, so that fits in with the established Anglican Church, though I did actually play a Catholic monk at one time, so it's really ecumenical.

BRIAN   But what about the Reverend Noot? He was the nice one.

DEREK   He was very nice. The trouble is that when you travel – and I've put on plays in about eighteen countries – wherever you go the professionally religious tend to look you up. And in Australia in particular, I think.

In Australia in 1971 when I first got there, I became frightfully chummy with Tommy Thomas, the Dean of Melbourne and a very keen cricket follower, because he lives just near the MCG. He was due to come over to England, and a few days before that I'd been doing some recordings for the Scripture Union on tape. Unfortunately I went on a television programme – it was a half-hour comedy with Rosemary Leach – and I had to put my toes in the water and say, 'This is bloody freezing', and suddenly people wrote saying how disgraceful it was that I, who was practically a professional priest, had said 'Bloody'. So I then had to withdraw from the Scripture Union. Three days later, my friend Tommy Thomas arrived, and I was driving him up to Lincoln to see the

Dean and, as we were going up the motorway he said, 'Oh, look over there, Derek, there's a bloody marvellous view.' And I said, 'Dean, I've been struck off the Scripture Union for saying that. You ought to be excommunicated.'

BRIAN   What about dear old Robertson Hare, who was in *All Gas and Gaiters* with you? He was sweet, wasn't he?

DEREK   Oh, sweet man, yes. He had rather an interesting war, too, you know – First World War. I remember asking him what he did in the war and he said, 'I was in the Bicycle Corps.' Well, he would be, wouldn't he?

I said, 'What did you do?' He said, 'We used to cycle against the Boche on our bicycles.' And my wife said, 'What happened if you were shot at?' He said, 'We used to take cover.' I said, 'Where?' 'Behind our bicycles,' he said. 'Then one day a terrible accident befell me. We were gathered on the parade ground at Ypres and the brigadier gave the order to mount bicycles and I mounted my bicycle and I landed on my left testicle, which then assumed enormous proportions and I was invalided out of the Bicycle Corps.' Well, it could only happen to him, couldn't it, really? I once told that story on New Zealand radio and they stopped the recording and said, 'You can't say things like that on radio.'

BRIAN   And you know you can't say things like that on *Test Match Special.*

DEREK   I remember when we finished the series of *All Gas and Gaiters* Robertson Hare was nearly ninety, and he was finding it a little difficult to remember the words. And he had to come in and say to the Bishop, played by Bill Mervyn, 'Excuse me, my lord, I want a bed for the night, urgently.' But in fact, with a studio full of people and the cameras turning, he came in and said, 'Excuse me, my lord, I want a bird for the night, urgently . . . oh dear, oh dear . . . oh calamity.'

BERNARD CRIBBINS

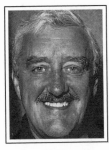

I INTRODUCED BER-
nard Cribbins, our
guest at the Lord's
Test match in
1986, as my wife
Pauline's favour-
ite comedian. He
was, and still is,
and we saw him recently playing a gangster disguised as a
clergyman in the hit musical *Anything Goes*. He was not
only very funny but also proved that he is no mean song-
and-dance man. I was not surprised about the singing
because his records *Right Said Fred* and *The Hole in the
Ground* have been favourites in my family for years.

He has the real advantage for a comedian of having a
funny face. It's difficult to look at him and not laugh at his
large expressive eyes. This makes it all the more remarkable that whenever I have seen him in the film of *The Railway Children* I have unashamedly cried at one or two
scenes. It means of course that he has what most of the
great comedians have – heart.

Mind you, you would never have guessed it if you had
been with us in the commentary box. He kept us in a per-
manent state of laughter, which was no mean feat consid-
ering what was happening out on the field. Whilst he was

with us India's last two batsmen were putting on 75 runs in 25 overs, thanks to a fine 126 not out by Vengsarkar.

LORD'S, 7 JUNE 1986

BRIAN JOHNSTON   When did you first take to cricket? Were you an infant prodigy?

BERNARD CRIBBINS   No, not at all. We used to chalk things on the wall in Oldham – they weren't stumps – just rude things we used to chalk on the wall. I got involved in cricket through Sid James and Peter Haigh. In the early sixties they got me into the Lord's Taverners and I started playing charity cricket for them, and I played until about eleven years ago when I bust my wrist and I don't want to play any more, because I cry if I fall over.

BRIAN   So what were your great attributes at cricket?

BERNARD   Ah, are you ready for this? My greatest joy, or the spectators' greatest joy, was seeing me walk out to the wicket, because I had a very funny walk. And it was even funnier on the way back. I think the greatest score I ever amassed was about 23 in a game with Harry Secombe over in Sutton or somewhere. I used to bowl a bit. I remember playing down at Portsmouth on the Combined Services Ground there. Kenny Barrington, another lovely man I got to know through cricket, was playing. He gave me the ball to bowl and I really didn't know what I was doing. And I was bowling to that very large gentleman, Fellows-Smith.

BRIAN   Oh, yes, Pom-Pom.

BERNARD   And he came up to me at the end of one of my overs and said, 'Every one of those was doing something.' He didn't say what. But I was trying. I just enjoyed it. I felt I should be able to play, but I'd never had any training, so I didn't know what I was doing.

BRIAN   Well, I bet you Fellows-Smith would have played you seriously and wouldn't try and get out. He was a great one for getting his three figures.

BERNARD   Kenny Barrington that day actually did score a ton.

BRIAN   Dear old Pom-Pom played in a charity match for me once and it was the sort of match where you got out if you got to 50, but he went plodding on and we were getting a bit fed up. We sent people in to run him out, and he ran *them* out. When he got to 98 we thought, well, we'll scupper him, we'll all get up and applaud, 'Well done! Marvellous hundred!' But he never even took off his cap. He scored two more runs and then gave his wicket away. He kept count, you see.

What other players did you play with in charity cricket? I think the great thing is they're kind to you, aren't they?

BERNARD   Yes, they are. If they see you're a total idiot, which I was at cricket, they don't bowl hard at you. They stick one down the leg side to get you off the mark. I played in a match with Sir Learie Constantine. He was lovely, because I'm from Lancashire and he used to play up there, not far from where I was born.

BRIAN   Nelson was his club.

BERNARD   So it was nice actually to be in the same dressing-room as him. The Bedsers I played with, Dave Halfyard and J.J. Warr, people like that. It's all going back a bit.

BRIAN   It makes us feel rather tall, doesn't it, changing in the dressing-room with all these great people. Have you ever played here at headquarters?

BERNARD   No, I haven't. I came along with my kit once for a Lord's Taverners' match – no, don't laugh – and I finished up selling raffle tickets. I wasn't picked. I think I was just too tall for that particular team.

BRIAN   You probably made more money than you would have made runs.

BERNARD   Probably yes, but I walked round with the blanket at least three times. I would love to have played here. I played at the Oval. I was in the middle there with Rachael Heyhoe-Flint. I got out for about six and she went on and got six hundred or something.

BRIAN   Were you here when Norman Wisdom played? He was playing and doing his falling over and things and a Member who had been asleep woke up and blinked and said, 'I don't know if that chap's a good cricketer, but he'd make a bloody fine comedian.'

BERNARD   I think the same Member is here today, because I was sitting out in the sunshine and an airship was going round the ground and this chap woke up and said, 'What's that bloody Zeppelin doing here?'

BRIAN   Do you think he'd been asleep since 1914?

BERNARD   Probably, yes. He must have noticed the new paintwork and things, mustn't he?

BRIAN   You've been seen in Australia recently. Did you see any cricket there?

BERNARD   Yes, three years ago I was in Adelaide when the team was there, and Robin Jackman, who's a friend of ours, got us into the dressing-room. It was rather nice to sit on the veranda with the chaps when it was all going on. One felt very honoured, I must say, as a non-cricketer.

BRIAN   Would you describe yourself as a comedian?

BERNARD   No, I'm a comedy actor. I do do funny things, but then I've done such a lot of things in this business.

BRIAN Do you dance at all?

BERNARD I move around a bit. One of the nicest things I've done in the forty odd years I've been in this game now was *Guys and Dolls* at the National Theatre about two years ago. That was an absolute joy.

BRIAN Which part did you play in that?

BERNARD I played Nathan Detroit. That really was a wonderful thing to have done and I had quite a bit of dancing to do in that. We had six weeks' rehearsal and the choreographer really put us through it. We finished with a two-and-a-half-minute tap routine which was knackering for an old gentleman like me.

BRIAN And did you end up with your hand facing out to the audience?

BERNARD Yes, we did all that. Totally traditional.

BRIAN The records you've made, which have sold millions, I should think, *Right Said Fred* and *The Hole in the Ground*, which one did you do first?

BERNARD The very first thing I did was called *Folk Song* which you probably can't remember now. It went, 'Upon the Monday morning-o, the rain it was a-raining.'

BRIAN Oh, yes . . . but go on.

BERNARD I can't remember the rest of it. That sold quite well, so they wanted another one and that's when *Hole in the Ground* was written and *Right Said Fred* followed that. When I was in Adelaide, Geoff Miller, the Derbyshire bowler, started to sing that at a party after the Test. And he said, 'I learnt that when I was a kid', which he did, of course, because it is twenty-two years old, but he'd learnt all the wrong words and he was singing something totally different.

BRIAN Were they better words than yours?

BERNARD No, they weren't, they were dreadful. I'm glad I can't repeat them.

BRIAN   In Australia you were in *Run for Your Wife*.

BERNARD   It was a play that I first did in Adelaide, and then we opened the Theatre of Comedy at the Shaftesbury Theatre with it. Richard Briers and I did that for six months there.

BRIAN   You're a founder member of the Theatre of Comedy.

BERNARD   I am, yes. It's been very successful indeed and it's brought together a good company of comedy actors. One of the nicer things that happened is that normally if you're going to Australia there's a ruling that Australian Equity only allows in one actor or maybe two at the most from England, and the rest of the company have to be Australian, which is fair enough. But last year we took out the whole company. There was an exchange deal and the other half of that has just happened.

BRIAN   That makes sense. Now, I know what role I liked

you best in. It was *The Railway Children*.

BERNARD   Yes, that was special.

BRIAN   It was a bit emotional at times. I blubbed a bit.

BERNARD   A five-handkerchief movie.

BRIAN   Was that fun to do?

BERNARD   Yes, smashing, because it was Lionel Jeffries' first venture as a director. He'd also done the screenplay, and he's an old friend and we had a lot of fun together on other films, and it was great to have him in charge of the whole production.

BRIAN   Was it actually done on a railway station, or was it a studio set?

BERNARD   No, we did a bit of studio stuff, but an awful lot of it was done on location in Yorkshire on the Keighley–Worth Valley Railway, which is a Steam Preservation Society, and we were up there for two weeks. Every day was sunshine, bit of cloud, bit of wind and it looked absolutely lovely. It was 1970. It's hard to believe, because it does seem like last year.

BRIAN   But how difficult is it for you, because people expect you to be funny, and you then have to put on a little bit of drama? Is that a difficult switch?

BERNARD   No, I don't think it is. If you're like me and you do more comedy than anything else, you become better at it obviously. And I really find comedy quite easy. The rest of acting is also quite easy for me. I'm a lucky person. I've also been at it a long time – forty-odd years – so I do know, without boasting, what I'm doing. But I find it quite easy to turn on the other emotion. I found the anger and anguish that Mr Perks went through in *The Railway Children* very real. It was well written. It was a nicely staged scene and that all helps to make it work.

BRIAN   You've got sad looking eyes, haven't you?

BERNARD   Well, I've just looked at the score, haven't I?

BRIAN   Do you have time to come and watch cricket?

BERNARD   No, I don't, quite honestly. I took part in a very silly game in a snowstorm in February once. It was for Bertie Joel. He has a charity match each year for Multiple Sclerosis. We played it on Kew Green in a blizzard. I umpired. I had on my fishing gear, waterproof trousers, a big Barbour coat, a mask like a balaclava and I looked like a terrorist. My feet were in wellies.

BRIAN   Did you give anyone out?

BERNARD   No, I didn't, because I couldn't see that far through the snow. I stood there with a bottle of Scotch in my pocket. I was the most popular person on that field.

BRIAN   Now, one thing I must finish with. I had a great friend who was a very good bowler and he bowled once for Middlesex. Sir Pelham Warner came up to him one day and said, 'Right, we'd like you to play for us for the rest of the season.' And he said, 'I'm very sorry, I can't. I'm going fishing.' Now, I think that would be a man after your own heart. Fishing is very dear to you is it not?

BERNARD   Last Sunday I was invited down to the River Avon in Wiltshire to fish a mayfly hatch. I'd never fished one. It's a phenomenon. It happens for about a week or two in the year, and you never see them again. The weather was a bit cold and a bit blowy, so therefore they weren't hatching, but I actually had twelve trout and five grayling all on a dry fly. The fishermen out there will know exactly what I'm talking about.

BRIAN   Is it all in the casting? Are you a good caster?

BERNARD   Yes. If you look at it in golf terms, I fish off about three.

BRIAN   What's the biggest fish you've ever caught?

BERNARD   I suppose a shark. I did five films over in Ireland on fishing, one of which was on shark fishing. I was paid to go and fish!

BRIAN   Also you have as a hobby fly-tying.

BERNARD   Yes, I tie flies. I caught my first salmon on one of my own tyings.

BRIAN   What do you use?

BERNARD   Feathers, tinsel, there are more and more artificial things coming into it now.

BRIAN   Do you make up your own colours?

BERNARD   You can invent one, but there are certain traditional things that copy an insect or a fish that you have to use, because that's what the trout are expecting to see. But occasionally you tie up something fancy, or something quite weird, and it does well for maybe a day or so, then suddenly they don't want to look at it.

JOHN CLEESE

I HAD ALWAYS wanted to meet John Cleese. He had made me laugh so much and so often in things like *Monty Python* and *Fawlty Towers*. And now of course he has become a star in the film world. Just to look at his dead-pan face makes me laugh. He has always been the supreme debunker of pomposity, and it has also been obvious that he is a very funny writer. But I was not sure whether in himself he was a funny man. His physical appearance is eye-catching with his height, and those incredibly loose and rubbery legs so hilariously displayed in his famous Ministry of Funny Walks.

I was also intrigued by the amazing acceleration and speed with which he could hurl himself upstairs in *Fawlty Towers*. Somehow he never banged his head nor injured himself as he rushed through those narrow doorways.

What I did know about him was that he was mad keen on cricket. From the moment he arrived in our commentary box on the third day of the Headingley Test in 1986, it became obvious how seriously he took his cricket. We were flattered that he had taken the trouble to drive up all the way from London just to be our guest, especially as he had to drive back again that afternoon for a concert in the evening.

Once settled at the back of the box, he watched every ball with a passionate intensity. He was clearly analysing each delivery, making whispered comments and asking astute questions to the 'experts' in the box. So I thought the best way to start was to find out his thoughts on cricket.

HEADINGLEY, 21 JUNE 1986

JOHN CLEESE   Well, I wish I spent a bit more time watching it, because I do get very intrigued by it. It's a wonderful game and I lost contact with it a few years after I stopped playing. I really stopped playing after Cambridge and anyway I never played for anybody good at Cambridge – just for my college.

BRIAN JOHNSTON *(an Oxford man)*   Is there anybody good at Cambridge?

JOHN   Oh, there were good ones at the time. It was Brearley's era more or less. But I went off to America and I lost contact. It's funny once you've been away from the game for two or three years, it takes a long time to get back in. I got back to England and didn't really get interested again until Somerset started winning matches. I grew up in the fifties when I think they got the wooden spoon seven years in a row.

BRIAN   With people like C.C. Case and J.C.W. McBryan.

JOHN   Well, no, that was before me. They were OK, but there was a time in the fifties when they used to win about one match a season, and I used to trot down to Taunton or Weston-super-Mare to watch them, and they were terrible, absolutely terrible.

BRIAN   But you're a great analyser, obviously, because the probing questions you were putting to us all earlier showed you were watching very carefully and trying to work things out.

JOHN   Well, yes. I find it is fascinating, endlessly fascinating.

BRIAN   Can we go back to when you first played cricket. How tall were you as a boy at Clifton?

JOHN   Well, I was too tall too soon. I was six foot when I was twelve, at my prep school in Weston-super-Mare, where I was coached by Bill Andrews.

BRIAN   What a character!

JOHN   That's right.

One of the difficulties of my cricket watching career was that I grew up with that extraordinary Somerset team of the late forties with people like Harold Gimblett and Arther Wellard and dear Bertie Bewes.

BRIAN   Bertie Bewes – he had a pub later.

JOHN   Oh, he was wonderful, with that extraordinary little hop, skip and jump run-up. And tiny little Johnny Lawrence and Harold Stephenson. I can't imagine a team so full of personalities and anything after that has always seemed less colourful.

BRIAN   To me the sad thing is that their cricket was fun, although they might not have done too well. Now, it's all you must win, and you get spectators who just want to see them win and do not really care about the characters or the type of cricket.

JOHN   But that's been a kind of continuing process as

long as I can remember. Winning has become progressively more important and once that happens sport loses something, doesn't it? The great moments of sportsmanship do send a kind of thrill round the crowd, because they're a reminder that what is bringing us together is greater than the need to defeat each other. That's why those great moments of sportsmanship are so touching and absolutely transform the atmosphere round the ground in a moment. But there's very little of that now because the idea that winning is more important than anything else has completely taken over.

BRIAN Let's go back to a twelve-year-old six footer. You could have been a demon fast bowler – the terror of the other schools.

JOHN I was physically weak and fragile. I was incredibly thin, so I used to run up quite a long way and then bowl slow, which was a good trick for the first ball. Also, it was only when I got to about the age of eighteen that I realised I needed a long bat, because the moment I picked the bat up I was literally overbalancing towards the off stump having been at too great an angle to start with.

BRIAN And when you went to Clifton, was the great Reg Sinfield coach?

JOHN Yes, and a marvellous coach too. In fact, although I was fond of several of the masters at Clifton, I think I got more from Reg than I did from any of the others. He was a terrific coach, but he also had a wonderful kind of wry humour and wisdom about him.

He went on coaching at Clifton for years after I left, and I remember him telling me that he was bowling fast to Bill Ponsford during the Australian tour of 1934.

BRIAN Yes, and I saw him – it dates me – in 1926 with Dipper, who went in first for Gloucestershire.

JOHN He bowled fast to start with and then off-spin.

BRIAN   Like Goddard.

JOHN   That's right, Sinfield one end and Goddard the other.

BRIAN   Did you have any other players who you particularly followed. The greats, like Hammond – he was before you – or Compton?

JOHN   I suppose Denis Compton was one, but funnily enough it was more that old Somerset team that caught my imagination, and I only began to lose interest after our fifth wooden spoon in a row. And then I seemed to get back into it, partly because the team of the late seventies actually started winning one or two trophies. I can still remember sitting at Lord's in 1979 when we won our first Gillette Cup. We'd been in the final the year before and lost to Sussex, and then finally we beat Northants. But it would never be the same. I actually sat there thinking, 'They've won something. They've actually won.' It was the first time they'd won anything in a hundred years and I felt it would never be the same again, the romance had gone out of it.

BRIAN   Did you ever captain a side?

JOHN   Yes, I captained my prep school team. I've got a photograph of myself walking off the field because at that time I was already over six foot and of course all the others were about four foot. It's an extraordinary picture.

BRIAN   I hope you don't mind analysing yourself a little bit. People think of you as irascible.

JOHN   Ah, but that's only since *Fawlty Towers*. What happens is that people form a kind of stereotyped image of you, depending on what was the last thing that you did. If you go back about twenty years to the time I started on the box with David Frost in 1966 – *The Frost Reports* with Ronnie Barker, Ronnie Corbett, Julie Felix, Tom Lehrer – in those days I was very much Frostie's sidekick, and people would expect me to be standing around by David Frost. Then shortly after that Python started, and then I was regarded as a great Kookie, zany, madcap. I can't remember what the other word was!

BRIAN   Very often the establishment figure who was being mocked, in pinstripe and bowler hat.

JOHN   But that's not what people remembered so much, although actually that is what I did. People thought of me as just being wild and unpredictable, but unfortunately I've never achieved that.

BRIAN   But in private life are you wild and unpredictable?

JOHN   No, I'm rather tame and predictable and boring actually. Slightly introverted, which surprises people; but you often find that people who are slightly shy and introverted are able to explode into action when they're given a socially sanctioned opportunity to do so, like being on the stage and damn well having to be extrovert.

BRIAN   You did a pretty useful Hitler – an unlikely Hitler at six-foot six or so.

JOHN   Yes, that Hitler sketch was one of my two or three favourites. I wrote it with Michael Palin.

BRIAN   I bet I know another one, the old dead parrot.

JOHN   The dead parrot I was fond of, and also the cheese shop.

BRIAN   Did you write those as well?

JOHN   Most of them. The Hitler one is the only one I think I ever wrote with Michael Palin, which was a great delight. But one of the disappointments of Python was that we always fell into patterns of writing with the same people. I think it would have been much more fun if we had mixed the writing up.

BRIAN   Did you all sit round a table as a sort of soviet of writers?

JOHN   Well, we used to sit around for about three days at the beginning of a series, and have lots of ideas and agree what we were going to write, and then go off and write completely different things. I think that was because once someone had thought of an idea there was then no hon-our in writing it. The prestige comes with thinking of the idea and writing it. Then we used to get together each week and read each other's material out. There was not a great deal of passion for cricket amongst the Python group.

BRIAN   But you used to do some sketches which took off me and Peter West once or twice. Who was the chap who put those in, because he obviously watched us very closely and took off all our mannerisms?

JOHN   Well, I'm afraid that was me. I'd forgotten that sketch. I think I wrote that originally for the radio and then I think we re-wrote it, as far as I remember, and we also had 'Pasolini's Test Match', which had naked cricketers writhing on the ground.

BRIAN Do you think that would improve cricket?

JOHN No, I like it staid.

BRIAN With the white flannels and all that. Let's hope they never wear shorts.

Now at Cambridge you got into the Footlights. Had you ever done any acting before? Why did you join the Footlights?

JOHN I don't really know. It's all very strange, because there's not a great deal of artistic activity in Weston-super-Mare, and certainly no one in my family or anywhere near it had ever been in entertainment or on the stage or anything like that. But I think it was something to do with being so tall, and also being an only child and therefore slightly reserved and capable of being on my own a lot without needing to seek out company. I think I found that when I first went to school I was a little bit of an outsider, and I think I discovered that by making people laugh I could get accepted more and become more popular.

I discovered I could get laughs, I remember quite distinctly, in form 2A in Mr Sanger-Davies' English lessons. He was a lovely man, who I'm afraid is no longer with us. But it was that particular moment that I started making jokes, and I remember that the class laughed, and I remember that it made me feel very good. It's actually a wonderful feeling to make people laugh. Everybody likes to tell jokes.

BRIAN I've tried for years and I haven't had the feeling yet!

Are you bored with being asked about *Fawlty Towers*? Do you mind people thinking of you as Basil Fawlty?

JOHN I think there's always a bit of you that would rather the audience thought that the writing and acting was an exercise in craft of some kind. But it is a funny thing, because John Howard-Davies, who produced the first several *Fawlty Towers*, warned me in advance when he realised the show was going to be a success. He said, 'You realise that now everybody will think that you are like Basil.' And I said, 'Will they really?' He said that it is always the case that straight actors are recognised as actors – nobody thinks that Laurence Olivier is going to be terribly jealous because he played Othello. People are going to say that his was a performance. But, he said, that if you do a successful comic character, like an Alf Garnett or one of the Richard Briers or Leonard Rossiter characters, then they always think that that's who you are. And I've noticed it's true, but it's only with comedy.

BRIAN When you used to hit poor Manuel, was that a false clap, or did you actually strike him once or twice?

JOHN Well, there are ways of faking it, but on one occasion I'm afraid, when I was hitting him with a saucepan, I didn't get the timing quite right, and dear old Andrew Sachs was a little bit out to lunch for two days.

BRIAN Now, you did twelve programmes.

JOHN That's right, only twelve, and do you know how long ago they were? 1975 and 1979.

BRIAN Any particular favourites – the one with the rat running loose?

JOHN The rat I was enormously fond of. The special effects department produced that rat and I almost kissed them. We got about sixty seconds out of that rat sitting in the biscuit tin. I loved the dead body one, and my favourite moment is in the one where he goes down to get the ducks from the restaurant. You remember, he drops the first one, gets the second and he's only got the blancmange. The best bit is when he takes the lid off and puts it straight back on, as though it might help the blancmange to go away. But when he lifts it up again, he actually looks in the blancmange – puts his fingers down into it – just in case there's a duck underneath!

BRIAN   Is it a fact that you might be writing some more, or is it curtains?

JOHN   No, Connie and I wrote them together and after we'd done the twelve we definitely felt that if we wrote any more we knew what the audience would say. They'd say that they'd enjoyed them, but that they weren't as good as the first two series. I don't think there was any way of getting round it. The second series was probably the best thing I'll ever do, which is why I don't come on television now, because if I do something that isn't as good, people will say, 'Ah, he's not as good any more.'

The only people who tell me they don't enjoy *Fawlty Towers* are hoteliers, who sit there for three minutes and suddenly they see what's going to happen. They see that the chef's going to get drunk, or there's going to be a dead body, and from then on they sit there in the most appalling state of nerves. But I can get that watching England play cricket or football normally – particularly football – there's no enjoyment in it at all.

BRIAN   Well, I hope you're going to spend the afternoon here with us.

JOHN   Oh yes, it's very nice to be asked, and also you do get the best view in England from this box. It's almost as good as on television.

TIM BROOKE-TAYLOR

IT WAS RAINING ON the Saturday of the Edgbaston Test in 1986 when Tim Brooke-Taylor was our guest. I remember this because he had just come up from the Henley Regatta where it had been even wetter. He always swears that when he and I met for the first time a good many years ago, I went up to him and said, 'Hello Brookers. We've never met. How are you?' A slightly unusual form of introduction I admit, but very probably true.

He is not in the usual run of comedians, having been educated at Winchester, sporting a double-barrelled name and coming from a family with a strong sporting background. He tends to belittle his ability, especially at cricket, where he is yet another Lord's Taverner, who turns out on Sundays in aid of charity. If you are a funny man, which Tim is, it is more or less impossible for you to try to play seriously in front of a crowd. But he has all the basic skills, and was obviously well coached at school.

He also claims to be nervous – even terrified – before appearing on a show. But listening to his brilliant ad libs in

I'm Sorry I Haven't a Clue you would never have guessed it. I must have seen Tim on TV more than most comedians because *The Goodies* was always a special favourite with my children. He obviously enjoyed his day with us. I suspect he enjoys almost everything he does.

EDGBASTON, 5 JULY 1986

BRIAN JOHNSTON   We're great ones for initials in the BBC and our guest today is known in the BBC by his initials – T.B.T. for Tim Brooke-Taylor – a great cricketer. You play a lot for the Lord's Taverners Tim, but are you qualified for the Primary Club? Have you ever been out first ball?

TIM BROOKE-TAYLOR   I remember my first game for the Taverners. It's very frightening if you're somebody like myself. I love cricket and I've made several centuries – in my bath. But to appear on a big cricket ground in front of a lot of people with some of your heroes, striding out to bat – or limping out – is frightening. The ball came down and it was a nice gentle one, but they had made the mistake of bowling it at the wicket, and between it passing my bat and hitting the stumps, the bowler's umpire and the square leg umpire both shouted 'No ball!' So I think I was denied my membership of the Primary Club.

BRIAN   Well, it's a great compliment, because it means the crowd had come to watch you and not the bowler. As a young boy how much cricket did you play?

TIM   As a young boy I was quite good up to about the age of fourteen or fifteen. I showed promise. My uncle and cousin played for Derbyshire and that was no mean feat in those days. And about the age of fourteen or fifteen I captained, at school, the Nawab of Pataudi amongst others.

BRIAN Was this at Winchester?

TIM Yes, that's right. And it all went wrong after that. About that age I lost my nerve, so I sympathise with any professional cricketer.

BRIAN What sort of captain were you?

TIM I was captaining the under-fifteens once, and we were playing the London Schools and they were viciously good and there was no chance of us winning, but there was a chance of us drawing. In the last over they needed four to win, and the obvious thing to do was to bowl outside the off stump and make sure they didn't score.

BRIAN Doing a Trevor Bailey.

TIM Exactly. A lot of people volunteered to bowl, but I thought I'd better do it. Anyway, the first three balls were wides. So, there were still six balls to go, and one run to get. It was the captain's bowling that cost the game, and I still have not got over the scars of that. For days I thought people were looking at me because of it.

BRIAN But you come from a great sporting family. I couldn't believe it when someone told me your grandfather was a great footballer.

TIM Yes, he played centre forward for England. He was also a parson.

BRIAN A parson playing centre forward for England. When would this have been?

TIM The 1890s . . . I met a very old man who said he'd seen him playing down in Cardiff, when he broke his leg, and that they could hear the crack all round the ground. He was splendid.

BRIAN And your mother?

TIM My mother played lacrosse for England. I'm rather

proud of that. That was in the 1920s.

BRIAN   Was there tremendous rivalry, with your grand-father saying, 'He must play football,' and your mother saying, 'He must play lacrosse,' so you chose cricket?

TIM   I think it was hoped that I was going to play what I wanted to play. It's like a lot of boys in mid-teens, there was a lot of expectation of you and how you were going to develop physically. A great deal of it is to do with nerve.

BRIAN   Are you nervous on the telly, or on the stage?

TIM   Absolute complete butterflies. I always work on that. Every time I've been really confident I've gone wrong. I know you make commentating seem easy, but I should think you probably get quite nervous. I do, always.

BRIAN   I'm told one ought to get nervous, but one waffles away. But you have to keep very much to scripts and not waffle.

TIM   There are two things I like. I like it well-scripted and well-rehearsed, or totally ad-libbed. It's the half-way in between, like – 'Tim, would you stand up and be very funny for ten minutes about the charity,' or whatever it is – that's the one I find very difficult. When I don't have a routine.

BRIAN   Do you mind being thought of as *The Goodies*? You've done so many other things probably more individ-ual. *The Goodies* appeared to be completely off the cuff, but obviously it wasn't.

TIM   Well, that's the highest compliment you can get. It was in fact very hard work. Most of the filming – where we looked silly running around in the country, usually pre-tending it was summer in India or somewhere – was really done when it was freezing cold, in February, somewhere in Britain, and you might have to do eight or nine takes.

BRIAN   I once rode a tandem, but you had a trandem! Now that must be impossible.

TIM   Yes. Especially if you're the one in front. The ones at the back don't care, but at the front you've got to steer. The first one – the mark one machine – had no freewheel and no brakes. It was one of those where you have to keep your feet on the pedals, and jam them backwards to brake. Bill Oddie, at the back, wasn't pedalling at all because it was a tandem made into a trandem, so he was wobbling from side to side. The first day, filming in Maidenhead, Graeme Garden and I had to go to hospital three times. We were going downhill with our legs astride.

BRIAN   What's the most difficult thing? Starting or stopping?

TIM   Starting. It was a great routine. We used to say, 'One, two, three, hup! Four, five, six', and into position, and go. Otherwise you couldn't get the momentum going. People thought we were kidding. The cameramen and lighting people thought we were showing off, but we couldn't do it any other way. It was very dangerous.

BRIAN   But it must have been great fun to do.

TIM   I'm a great believer in working in teams for comedy. I think it's a great shame when people produce good comedy teams and then somebody whispers in an ear, 'Look, you're the best. You go solo.' I think solo comedy is not so much fun.

BRIAN   We had old Cleesers in the other day and he said that you were one of the boys with him at Cambridge.

TIM   We studied law together. We actually revised together for our law finals.

BRIAN   How many were there in the revue?

TIM   In the 1963 revue there were, John Cleese, Graham Chapman, Graeme Garden, myself, Bill Oddie, David Hatch – now boss to all of us, he's become God (Managing Director Network Radio) – Eric Idle, Trevor Nunn directed us, and I've missed several people out.

BRIAN   Did you play cricket at Cambridge?

TIM   I played quite a bit. I played for the Pembroke Second Eleven and then occasionally for the First Eleven. Unfortunately I didn't qualify for the Primary Club but I did for the Secondary Club.

BRIAN   Who were your cricket heroes?

TIM   Well, I am a Derbyshire man, and I used to go to the Derby nets for coaching, and Jackson and Gladwin were there and bowled at me. Cliff Gladwin knew how to get me every time and he would say, 'Come on, Les, come and have a go at this.' And I just never saw the ball. It wasn't speed, it was just sheer brilliance and they just had great fun destroying the confidence of this young lad. Then they would put me back.

BRIAN   And your Derby connections were not just cricket but football too weren't they?

TIM   Yes, I was a director of Derby County for a time. It was a tough time.

BRIAN   Did they go in the right direction?

TIM   They stayed more or less where they were. It's not one of the nicest moments of a Saturday afternoon sitting in a directors' box with fourteen thousand people pointing at you, shouting, 'What a load of rubbish.' It's not a thing you do for fun.

BRIAN   I have a book in front of me called *Tim Brooke-Taylor's Cricket Box*.

TIM   Willie Rushton, with whom I do *I'm Sorry I Haven't a Clue* on the radio, said, 'What's the name of your cricket book?' I said, '*Tim Brooke-Taylor's Cricket Box*.' And, quick as a flash, he said, 'Hmm, can't be much in that.'

BRIAN   I like the picture in it of the umpire in dark glasses. What's your opinion on umpires?

TIM   I am very pro cricket umpires. I've asked a lot of players what they think of umpires and they have enormous respect for them – unlike in any other sport – because they're usually ex-players, aren't they?

BRIAN   I think in other countries you find very few Test players who become umpires.

TIM   I asked Nick Cook about it and I thought he might have reservations, but he was very loyal and said, 'No, they're very professional here.'

BRIAN   Well, the great thing is that they know what's going on, and if someone is transgressing they draw him aside and say, 'Look, cut that out.' They don't wag fingers, and there's no notebook and pencil to take names.

Have you played much this season?

TIM   No, I turn out more for golf these days. I played a few weeks ago with a Spanish golfer at Woburn, and it was a Texas scramble, where you all drive off and you choose the best drive. Seve's wasn't up to mine, so he said, 'Captain, you take over.' So we took my drive.

BRIAN   That must have been a great moment.

TIM   I actually wanted to retire from life. When you've

seen my golf you know what an unlikely thing it was.

BRIAN   I've got a theory about golf. I do one or maybe two good shots in a round, and those are the ones I remember. Our opponents play only one or two bad shots in the round, and those are the ones they remember, and they're miserable!

TIM   That's right. Seve – my chum – hit a wonderful shot and I said, 'Great shot!' And he said, 'No it's a good shot, not a great shot.' And the next one I hit wasn't bad for me and he said, 'Good shot!' And I said, 'It was a great shot.' He said, 'No, it was a good shot.' And after he hit another and I said, 'That IS a great shot,' he said, 'Yes that is a great shot.' I said, 'Well, thank goodness you've admitted it.' And he said, 'You've got to understand, I hit three great shots a week.' And that is the standard he's thinking of. Since I played with him he hasn't lost a tournament. I think there might be a coincidence there.

A thing I wish I'd done in my book is scoreboards. The one at Lord's makes me very cross.

BRIAN   The scoreboard operators here at Edgbaston are very good.

TIM   They're very good scorers and operators, but I find it very difficult to know what has happened at any time.

BRIAN   Well, no, you've got to learn where all the things are on any scoreboard.

TIM   Why?

BRIAN   It's a good question. But it makes it more exciting. You go to every ground and you find something different. The last player on one is the number of the bowler on the next.

TIM   You were very helpful on our radio programme (*I'm Sorry I Haven't a Clue*) when we were going into the rules of 'Mornington Crescent'. You commentated on one of the greatest games of 'Mornington Crescent' I think probably ever played.

BRIAN   This 'Mornington Crescent', whose idea was it?

TIM   It goes back a long time now. I think it's first mentioned in the Domesday Book. I think they're repeating the documentary. Ken Livingstone made a very good point on that programme, I think, about how every tube line should have a Mornington Crescent. It was unfair that only the Northern Line had one.

BRIAN   How much preparation or warning do you get of things in *I'm Sorry I Haven't a Clue*?

TIM   About twenty per cent we're warned of. In fact, some of the best things are not prepared at all. I was listening to it in the car once and had to drive into a field, I was laughing so much, not when we were clever, but because I could actually hear myself sweating. There was an awful poem which would come towards you from someone else. When Humphrey Lyttelton pressed the buzzer you had to add the next line, and he would press it when he felt that there was a rhyme you could not do.

There's a story, shall we say, about an imp that lived in Edgbaston. You're desperately thinking how you're going to rhyme with Edgbaston, then he's got an orange and you've got to rhyme orange with something.

BRIAN   But are you quick on that? You must have the gift for it.

TIM   I'm the worst of the four of us. I think why the programme works – and it has actually worked very well – is because we haven't been trying to outdo each other. We're all trying desperately to keep the balls in the air. Willie Rushton, when he's on a good streak, is just the most miraculously funny man.

BRIAN   Yes, he can talk more sensible nonsense than anybody, can't he?

TIM   I think my favourite medium is radio, especially for

comedy. Because you can play any character. In the programme, *I'm Sorry I'll Read That Again*, I used to play Lady Constance deCoverlet, the dog called Spot and Tim Brown-Windsor, and they'd all talk to each other, and I used to get that very wrong.

BRIAN   In all these things you've always been made very pukka. In *The Goodies* you were always the pukka one.

TIM   Well, we had three roles, and they were almost the political roles. I was the Tory, Graeme the Alliance and Bill was somewhere left of . . . anywhere that's left. I won't go into it, but we weren't like we were, shall I put it that way. I actually slightly object when people assume you are the upper-class twit that your double-barrelled name would suggest. I worked in Italy for a time and they couldn't get used to it. They used to call me Tim Buk-Tu, which I thought was rather nice.

BRIAN   Well, Tim Buk-Tu, it's time that we had a little lunch.

JULIAN BREAM

WE HAD ALWAYS heard that Julian Bream was devoted to cricket, but until his visit to the commentary box we had never realised how deeply he loved the game. Not just as a spectator or listener, but also as a player. Here was a world famous guitarist at the top of his profession willing to risk his whole career by playing regularly for the local team!

Julian has travelled all over the world with his guitar – with Australia as one of his favourite destinations – mainly because he was able to watch some cricket there. As well as being an acknowledged master of the guitar he has been largely responsible for the revival of interest in Elizabethan lute music, on which he has done much research, and indeed he is acknowledged as the world's foremost lutenist.

How he ever found time to play cricket I don't know, but it once again shows how cricket attracts the artiste, be he musician, singer or actor. I asked when it first attracted him.

LORD'S, 26 JULY 1986

JULIAN BREAM   It happened at school. I was batting with another boy, and I actually saw him score a century from the other end. I scored three in that time, while he shielded me from the bowling, and I was so overwhelmed with the heroics of it all that it overtook my enthusiasm, and since then I've been absolutely crazy about cricket. I really learned by watching that innings. It was thrilling.

BRIAN JOHNSTON   But your fame has spread a bit more as a bowler. Have you been mostly a bowler?

JULIAN   Mostly a bowler – and so was that chap who I was talking about – Robert Hurst. He went on to play for Middlesex as a slow left arm bowler.

BRIAN   Oh, yes, Bob Hurst.

JULIAN   But I was always very keen on bowling. I love bowling.

BRIAN   And I expect you've got quite a few overs in, because you've captained your own side, haven't you.

JULIAN   I live out in Semley, which is on the borders of Dorset and Wiltshire, and we had a little village team. I say we had, because I can't play any more since I had a motoring accident a couple of years ago. But we used to play the next parish on a beautiful ground, which was an old country house cricket ground. A lovely setting, and my team was composed mostly of artists – painters, musicians and so forth – and the other team was largely retired colonels and farmers, and we used to have a few boys from the village just to run around the boundary.

BRIAN   So you captained the side. What sort of bowler were you?

JULIAN   I always tried to bowl leg-breaks and googlies. I could bowl reasonable leg-breaks at times, but rather dreadful googlies. I found it was a rather difficult ball to bowl.

BRIAN   Very important to have a good wicket keeper. Who was your wicket keeper?

JULIAN   Well, the wicket keeper was my agent, actually.

BRIAN   So he took fifteen per cent of the balls? And you picked up a few wickets from stumpings and things like that?

JULIAN   Well, largely from big hits into the outfield actually. I always had a very defensive field. I used to send all my men out, but I also used to pick the right end of the pitch. If I saw weeds growing at one end, I would bowl from the other end and hope to get the ball to pitch in the weeds.

BRIAN   People are going to say, with you a guitarist, what about your hands? I'm looking at them now. First of all, they are very small, so it must have been difficult to get your fingers round the ball.

JULIAN   I've never had difficulty getting them round the ball. I've sometimes had difficulty getting them round the guitar.

BRIAN   But they are small, aren't they? Do most guitarists have longer fingers than yours, or isn't it an essential?

JULIAN   I would have thought it is an essential thing. But I've got supple fingers, put it like that.

BRIAN   What about batting? Twenty-seven professionals have broken fingers this season. Have you ever been hit on the fingers?

JULIAN   Only once, and that was when I was about

fifteen. But I take great care with my hands and any risks that I take in the field or when batting are sort of calculated. If I think it's going to be a blinding catch I make an effort, but I'm actually miles away from the ball.

BRIAN Where did you put yourself in the field? It's no good being at slip.

JULIAN I used to like fielding at point or gully, that sort of area.

BRIAN Now, you've got fairly long nails. Wasn't there a danger of those being broken?

JULIAN Oh, always. The whole thing was really a very risky business, playing cricket, but I've never broken a nail.

BRIAN But you are a classical guitarist. Do you actually use only your nails? There's a thing called a plectrum which ordinary people use.

JULIAN Oh, that's rather impure, really. For the classical guitar we use either the fingers – you can use the ends of the fingers, the fleshy part – or the nails, but most players these days use their fingernails. And that's quite a bore, because you've really got to look after them and make sure they're nicely filed and polished.

BRIAN But in ordinary life, do you wear gloves to protect them?

JULIAN Not often. I somehow manage to have good fortune when it comes to fingernails. I'm just lucky that way.

BRIAN But supposing you do happen to break one, can you put on a falsie?

JULIAN I've tried that, but they tend to fly out into the audience.

BRIAN A bit dangerous if you're in the front row.

JULIAN People get very upset, you know. They ask for their money back.

BRIAN But do you carry false ones with you?

JULIAN   I have a box in my guitar case, yes.

BRIAN   When did you actually begin to take the guitar seriously?

JULIAN   I suppose when I was about fourteen or fifteen. In those days the guitar wasn't taken seriously by anyone, that was the problem. It was an instrument that was OK for folk music or jazz, but for classical music there was no possibility. There was no opening for a career on the classical guitar.

However, I was very fortunate because I played the piano and the cello a little bit, and I went to the Royal College of Music and studied those instruments and I just kept my guitar playing on the side. Then, finally, I had to earn a living and I just about earned enough money to keep going. But I was on the bread line. Then eventually the guitar became more popular and in the last twenty years it's become very popular, the classical guitar. But it says something, in a sense, for doing what other people don't do. If you hang around long enough you may get there. It's like being a leg-break bowler today.

BRIAN Now you've had an interest in developing the guitar.

JULIAN I used to have a workshop which housed different instrument makers, and I had a lute maker and a guitar maker there, and I've always been interested in the design of these instruments. The guitar is a very simple instrument. It just has six strings and it's really like a large cigar box with a hole in the middle, but there's a whole lot of technology about its design, which I find very fascinating. I call it technology, because nobody really knows how it works or why it should work.

BRIAN Do you have to use special woods?

JULIAN Certainly, special wood, and mature, high quality wood at that. But it's the interior construction – all the struts and spars – which are so critical in guitar making, and then the type of construction, and indeed the placement of these bars that give each instrument its special characteristic.

BRIAN How far does the guitar go back?

JULIAN It must go back to the eighth or ninth century. It's a Moorish instrument. There are some theories that the guitar was brought to Spain when the Moors invaded, but I have a feeling that the guitar was always in Spain. It is a very ancient instrument.

BRIAN And did you have a special musician that you followed or worshipped?

JULIAN Oh, yes indeed. The great Spanish guitarist, André Segovia. He was the one that really made the guitar popular. I had a difficult time, but he had a much more difficult time than me. It was, in fact, hearing an old record of his that really convinced me that it was the

94

classical guitar that I wanted to play, because when I was very young – ten or eleven – I used to play the plectrum guitar – the jazz guitar. My father brought home this marvellous record of Segovia playing and I heard it and I was enchanted, entranced and I realised that that was what I wanted to do.

BRIAN   You've done so many recordings, and I gather that you record locally. Do you have your own studio?

JULIAN   Well, you might think it is. It's a very, very beautiful baroque chapel set in the countryside about two miles from my home. It has the most wonderful acoustics. And that's why I use it. I can record there and the sound that you hear on the record is the pure sound of that chapel. I'm very fortunate that I happen to have that on my doorstep, and it's such an elegant and beautiful place.

BRIAN   Are you a six-hour-a-day practiser?

JULIAN   Five. I do five hours every day. This is the first day that I haven't actually practised the guitar.

BRIAN   You didn't have a go before breakfast this morning.

JULIAN   Well, actually, I did. I had a little go. But this is the first day I haven't actually done five hours practice for probably a month. I'm so keen on cricket that I can actually practise my exercises and listen to your commentary at the same time. I think the cricket commentary is some of the very best radio there's ever been.

BRIAN   Do you ever come to Lord's to watch?

JULIAN   Oh yes, I come quite often. In fact I sometimes come to a county match when I'm up in London. I travel up early in the morning and get a lot of business done, and then about teatime I come in to a county match and I love it. Partly because you can get a glass of beer out of hours, and also because it's so peaceful after the hurly-burly of London. Mind you I'm very saddened by the fact that very few people come to watch county matches. I always come on the Thursday of the Lord's Test with a very old and dear Jesuit friend of mine, who, incidentally, gives me permission to record in the chapel. He loves cricket and was a cricket coach for some time. When I had my team, and we had our matches at Semley, he would be my umpire.

BRIAN   Sir Julian Cahn used to have his own butler as his umpire.

JULIAN   A butler is all very well, but you must have a Jesuit priest because nobody ever questions his decisions. They wouldn't dare.

BRIAN   Have you had any amusing experiences at Lord's?

JULIAN   I remember last year, or maybe the year before, England won the toss and were batting. I don't think we were doing very well, because I do remember that Ian Botham came in about two overs before tea. The crowd gave him a tremendous cheer, and there was that extraordinary expectancy that accompanies him when he walks to the wicket. And he hit, what I thought, was a streaky four down to the third man boundary, and then went in to tea. I was needing a pee, but it was very crowded in the gents, so I waited until the first over after tea. It was still crowded then and we were all queueing up to go. There were six of us in line. The urinals there are very resonant, because they're made of metal, and the sound in there was quite incredible. Suddenly someone at the back said, 'Botham's out!' There was silence – and we all stopped – . . . and then the dribbles started again.

BRIAN   What a wonderful story.

Now, you travel a lot. Do you like that?

JULIAN   Well, it's part of the job. If you're any good, as I hope I am, you must broadcast your abilities. You can't just sit in Semley, Wiltshire. In fact I do the old-fashioned season, which is October to April and then I stop, because the cricket season starts.

BRIAN   Rather like Trevor Howard, who wouldn't film when there was a Test Match on.

JULIAN   That's right. I try and fit in the work around Test Matches, too. But last year from October to April I went round the world twice. I played all over America, Japan, Taipei, Hong Kong, New Zealand, Australia and Europe.

BRIAN   Do you have a hero amongst cricketers?

JULIAN   When I was a boy Denis Compton was always everybody's hero. He was just a tremendous player. And then I always loved Len Hutton's batting. I just thought it was so classical and wonderful. But these days, do we have hero types?

BRIAN   It's funny this association of cricket and music. There was dear old Neville Cardus and there was Sir John Barbirolli, who was mad on it, and one person you might not know about, Keith Miller, who used to slip away in the evenings to classical concerts when he was on tour. You'd often find him at the Albert Hall.

JULIAN   I admired him tremendously. It is interesting to note the number of musicians who are really interested in cricket. I don't know why it is, but there is definitely a relationship. I don't know if it's the time element in cricket that's so fascinating – you don't get that in one-day cricket – but it's what happens and how it develops and in musical composition that seems similar to me.

WILLIE RUSHTON

IN THE DAYS WHEN music-hall and variety were flourishing the best ad-libber on the stage was undoubtedly Tommy Trinder. He did not have an act as such, but relied on being heckled by the audience, and then putting the heckler down with a devastating retort.

Now the best and wittiest ad-libber on either television or radio today is Willie Rushton. The producers love him. He never lets them down. With his gruff voice he will come out – quick as lightning – with an outrageous *double entendre* at just the right moment. His timing is perfect and his speed of thought remarkable. No wonder he has been on almost every quiz or comedy show ever broadcast. This includes Radio 4's *Trivia Test Match* where he captains one side, and Tim Rice the other. I am the unfortunate chairman who has to try to keep control whilst trying to stop laughing.

Willie is a versatile chap, a brilliant cartoonist, writer, speaker and a loyal member of the Lord's Taverners, for whom he opens the batting. He never seems to be in a hurry. He has a slow shambling gait with long strides, and this tempo is reflected in his batting.

It would be untrue to describe him as smart. He normally wears an old bush hat, no tie, gaudy shirt, leather jacket, jeans – that sort of thing. Topped off, of course, by his beard. I was therefore amazed to see him so neat and tidy when he came up to our commentary box at the Oval during the third Test against New Zealand in 1986.

Before commenting on his appearance, I thought I had better humour him by referring to his prowess as a batsman.

THE OVAL, 23 AUGUST 1986

WILLIE RUSHTON   I've never knowingly made a nought actually, which is why I'm not wearing a Primary Club tie. At least I can't remember ever having made a nought, nor can I remember having dropped a catch.

BRIAN JOHNSTON   They tell me your memory is not what it was.

WILLIE   It's not what it was. There's a very useful part of the brain that dies as you grow older.

BRIAN   But can you explain your dress today? You've got a tie on!

WILLIE   I have a tie on. This is the Oval. I've been coming here for thirty-five years or so. I'm a member. I joined when I was thirteen and I always wear a tie.

BRIAN   Is it still what it was in the Long Room do you think?

WILLIE   Gone off a lot. There was man down there today with a haversack. Even I, who have been voted second worst-dressed man in Britain (Billy Connolly won – quite rightly in my view – but I was second worst, ahead of Harry Secombe. I don't know why Harry Secombe, but he'd just bought new clothing – he'd lost a lot of weight – and he looked like a tent, flapping in the wind), would never wear a haversack in the Long Room. That is going too far. Then another man came in who looked as though he'd been jogging, and I thought I'd go upstairs to the Radio box where they're decent. People dress properly for Radio, have you noticed? Television's absolute rubbish.

BRIAN   Well, you've got a Lord's Taverners' tie on.

WILLIE   And my Surrey county sweater, because it was so cold this morning, and I'm pretty neat.

BRIAN   Tell us how your cricket career started. You were educated at that well-known rowing school, Shrewsbury.

WILLIE   Yes, but I'm unable to swim. Therefore I couldn't row. It was a reasonable excuse. Classy drowning is my *métier*. But I've been very heavily into cricket since I was a child. I loved it. I wasn't very good, but I had coaching. You wouldn't believe that, but I actually went to Lord's twice when I was about twelve or thirteen. I had Jim Sims, the tall off-spinner, one year.

BRIAN   You probably played him as an off-spinner, which is why you couldn't hit him. He was actually a leg-spinner.

WILLIE   I don't think I got bat to ball for the entire eight pounds' worth. Then, next year, it was a wonderful man called Reg Routledge. He played for Middlesex quite a few times and was an absolute sergeant major who would say all the stuff about 'Keep the left arm up', and he taught us rigid off drives. Then I saw him make a hundred against Surrey which was quite the most chaotic innings I've ever seen in my life – the cow-shot was heavily employed – I learned that from him.

BRIAN Yes, he wasn't orthodox. He used to come in about seven or eight.

WILLIE And scored very quickly!

BRIAN You take batting quite seriously, don't you?

WILLIE Not any more. Not since I discovered that I had about eight blind spots, instead of one or two. The straight ball on the middle stump, for instance, has always been my downfall. But then about eight more occurred and I realised there was no point in worrying about it any more.

BRIAN So have you always supported Surrey since you were a young boy?

WILLIE My grandfather was a member of Surrey. He was a member of MCC and Lancashire as well, but he used to bring me here mainly.

BRIAN Who were your heroes?

WILLIE I think my major hero was Bernard Constable. He was a small swarthy man – slightly Arabian in looks, but a wonderful player – down the wicket to spin bowling like nobody's business, and he used to dress in cream. He was always different from everyone else. As the years go by he seems to have got yellower in my memory. I now see him like a sort of small canary. He's gone almost bright yellow now, but I think in fact it was just that he was cream and everyone else was white. He was magnificent and I don't know why he never toured for England.

BRIAN He was quite an amusing chap in the dressing-room.

WILLIE I believe so, but you never get that when you're watching. If only the fielders would speak up when they make good jokes.

Another lovely man was Geoff Whittaker, who used to go in about seven or eight and hit trams. I think his main aim in life was to whack it out of the ground and try to take a tram with him. I think that's why they abolished trams.

BRIAN   I think we must explain that the old Harleyford Road here, which now only has Henry Blofeld's buses, used to have the old trams going down it.

WILLIE   Yes, I can remember them. It was the noise as much as anything, that wow, wow, wow as they went past. And they used to slow down so that people could stand up in them just to watch. Two minutes of a Test Match and then off, back up towards town.

BRIAN   Well, looking at it now, is the Oval your favourite ground?

WILLIE   I think it is. I'm very fond of it. It's a good working cricket ground. Lord's you always feel is a sort of office block as well. A lot of people who go there have gone mainly for meetings or social events in boxes and that sort of thing, whereas everybody comes here just to watch the cricket. I think that's a good sign. I'm very fond of the gasometers, I don't know why. How can you be fond of a gasometer? But there they are and I'm very fond of them.

BRIAN   There are those little ones which go down. The big one always stays up which is very strange.

WILLIE   I don't want to hear about your private life.

BRIAN   How do you describe yourself – a cartoonist? Is that number one?

WILLIE   That's on my passport. I suppose that's the one place where you reveal yourself, rather more than in *Who's Who* where you lie a lot. And I have actor stroke cartoonist in my passport.

BRIAN   Which actor strokes a cartoonist?

WILLIE   I could give you a few names . . .

I think that covers most things. The acting is anything I say; the spoken word. And the cartooning is anything I write or draw. Even my distinguished novel – which is still available, I'm happy to say, at the Oval bookshop – which was 288 pages long, and I still think of it as a very long caption to a cartoon.

BRIAN   Were your cartoons started for children?

WILLIE   I've done some kids' books. I never did serious drawing. The War was on when I was a lad and I think I just started drawing humorous faces. The human face is a wonderful thing. You have a wonderful face, Brian.

BRIAN   Thanks, old man.

WILLIE   Could be captured instantly on paper.

BRIAN   I'd loathe to see the result.

WILLIE   It's a marvellous face to watch.

I've always doodled. When I came out of the Army I didn't know what to do and I went into a solicitor's office for a year, until exams loomed, and in their vaults they still apparently have conveyances and pink-tied documents covered in my drawings of mad conservative majors with red faces and moustaches, shouting.

BRIAN   You concentrate on faces more than anything else.

WILLIE   I have to draw the rest of the body now as well, but it's always been the human face that's fascinated me. I've never yet drawn anything, however bizarre, that I haven't usually met about three days later. You can't go too far with the human face.

BRIAN   So you produce life on paper.

Was there a nice art master at Shrewsbury who taught you?

WILLIE   A very, very good man. What I liked about him was that he saw the way I was going and never said, 'you must go back to drawing boxes or learning to paint land-scapes', or that sort of thing. He just encouraged me to do what I was best at, which was black and white cartoons.

BRIAN   Didn't you also edit a newspaper at Shrewsbury?

WILLIE   Yes, we had a magazine there called *Salopian*,

because of the classical upbringing. It got quite jolly when we did it. Richard Ingrams was on it at the same time.

BRIAN Ingrams – was he a good cricketer?

WILLIE Not bad. A very tall wicket keeper, rather like you. They're a very strange breed, tall wicket keepers. They're quite different from short wicket keepers.

BRIAN They let more byes through, because they can't stoop.

WILLIE They look like giraffes feeding.

BRIAN Was this then the start of *Private Eye*, you and Ingrams together?

WILLIE Yes. Christopher Booker, who was also in at the beginning of *Private Eye* (a very distinguished journalist now, having gone straight), and Paul Foot, who'd gone as far left as the Liberal Party then. He was still on his way left (I don't know how far left he is now; I think he's a Leninist Trotskyite Maoist at the moment, but he was moving into the pink area then) – the four of us were on the magazine at the same time, and it was virtually the same team that started *Private Eye* four or five years later.

BRIAN What was it then, just a little sheet or a few pages?

WILLIE We did three try-outs, which were just sort of grubby yellow sheets, about six pages stapled together. The person who put up the money was a nice man called Andrew Osman, who later became a novelist. He put up eight hundred quid, which was all we needed to start, and he also provided an enormous number of debs, who could stick labels on and lick stamps and do stapling. They were no use for anything else – they couldn't type or read or write – but they were wonderful for stapling and going out on London's bridges and selling copies. We did three of those yellow numbers, and then in the new year, 1962 I suppose – it goes back a bit – we brought out number four, which was officially number one. It took off, and we were

lucky that the *Observer* and several other newspapers picked it up, and it was away.

BRIAN   You're not responsible for paying some of the libel things yourself are you?

WILLIE   I've always avoided it. I've never had shares in *Private Eye*, which is a very dangerous area to be in I think. Although I'm self-employed, I've always tried not to have money in any venture in which I was involved. This has been quite a wise decision looking back over the years.

BRIAN   But you've worked a great deal for the BBC in more or less everything. How did you get into quiz shows? Every quiz we switch on now we're apt to hear Rushton.

WILLIE   It's not as bad as it was, because I suddenly realised it was getting out of hand. The quiz games multiplied as the BBC realised that it was a very cheap way of doing shows – no script – you don't have to pay writers.

I don't do as many as I did, but I was utterly happy to do

the *Trivia Test Match* with you. I always enjoy it. I don't think quiz games harm anybody, and they do allow you to fool around a little. But it got a bit out of hand after *Celebrity Squares.* I did about 130 of those. And it introduced me to a viewership. Normally I'd been going on at 11 o'clock at night or midnight. Whenever the swimming at Cardiff Baths ended, I'd find myself on television.

BRIAN Then it was *I'm Sorry I Haven't a Clue* on the radio.

WILLIE With Brooke-Taylor, Cryer, Junkin and co. and Humphrey Lyttelton.

BRIAN It sounds absolute chaos. Can you reveal how much warning you get beforehand of what you're going to have to do?

WILLIE It would be fair to reveal that over fifty per cent is ad-libbed, which isn't bad, I mean that's terrifying enough. Things like the ad-lib poem, we don't know where we're going, or when it will stop, or how. That's one of the hardest parts. We record a lot more than actually goes out. There's heavy editing.

BRIAN An ad lib from you might be a bit debatable sometimes.

WILLIE Certainly, but there are several of us. I am not the only one with the lively *double entendre* at hand. It gets quite filthy on occasions, but the audience like it. It's a good night out at the Paris. Several members of our audience are quite toothless, but gums howl with glee.

BRIAN It's amazing that audience at the Paris. There are regulars who wait outside in the rain.

WILLIE It's a great, free night out. After all we do two shows and that takes about two hours. So they get a two-hour free show up in the West End, and it's warm and comfortable.

Occasionally you get a charabanc load of Polish sailors who think it's a strip joint, and can't understand why the

British find two men sitting on either side of a stage is somehow sexually stimulating.

BRIAN Now what about that excellent book of yours, *W.G. Grace's Last Case?*

WILLIE It did very well. It's what I laughingly refer to as my first novel. It was actually nothing of the sort, but it was quite a jolly story, based roughly on *The War of the Worlds* which I always thought was the best sci-fi ever written. And at the end of it H.G. Wells said they'd be coming back, so I wanted something with *The War of the Worlds* continuing. I rather liked the idea of London after this war, with W.G. Grace playing at Lord's, and seeing the distant ruins and going down Park Lane which still hadn't been rebuilt.

BRIAN What sort of man do you imagine W.G. Grace was?

WILLIE Some of the critics said they thought I got him right. He was a fine bluff straightforward medical man, with not much knowledge of medicine. I gather the MCC tried to buy him a practice. I'm not sure that he had much of one. He probably kept his box on the surgery wall as a sort of conversation piece.

BRIAN What sort of face do you imagine he had behind all that beard?

WILLIE Well there are pictures of his early life aren't there? He was a fine square-jawed young man. They all had square jaws then, like Jessop. Maybe it was something to do with the photographic processes in those days.

Incidentally, my grandfather actually bowled Jessop.

BRIAN Where?

WILLIE Up in Lancashire. He used to play for Wigan. Opened the bowling for Wigan as a lad, my grandfather – Bertie Rushton. Not unknown over a bottle of Scotch in several clubs.

BRIAN   Did he bowl from the Pier End?

WILLIE   Both ends at the same time, I believe. He monopolised the side to some degree. He also opened the batting.

BRIAN   How did he get Jessop out?

WILLIE   The story he told me, after about three gins, was that Jessop had been in making quite a few, so my grandfather went up to the captain as a callow lad and said, 'Let me have a go, sir. I can take him.' And second ball he bowled him.

BRIAN   And since then the Rushtons have never looked back in the cricket world.

WILLIE   The Jessops have never spoken to us since. There's been this constant feud between Gloucestershire and Wigan.

BRIAN   Now you've also been to Australia. Did you travel round?

WILLIE   I have to admit I am responsible for the whole Packer business.

BRIAN   What?

WILLIE   Now it can be revealed. His father, Sir Frank Packer, owned Channel Nine television and most of the newspapers, and was a robber baron generally. I organised a game of cricket between what we laughingly called *Private Eye*, which was in fact a number of members of a magazine called *Oz*, and Channel Nine, for which Kerry Packer insisted on playing. Now, they'd never had a game of one-day cricket in Australia then, particularly not a beer match, which could be stopped every six overs for refreshment. And I also introduced the six-ball over there, because the old eight-ball over wouldn't have done – I mean, forty-eight balls between drinks – and Mr Packer thoroughly enjoyed it all. He thought it was a splendid day out, and I like to think the seeds were sown of the terrifying Packer years.

BRIAN   So in fact you're the chap we've all been looking for.

WILLIE   He left out the drinks break, though, which was actually the best bit. The man has no taste whatsoever. He also bowled bouncers at my twelve-year-old stepson. We agreed that he was not a man one would care to ask to tea.

BRIAN   You've got a lot to answer for if you're responsible for all those one-day matches England have to play when they go to Australia.

WILLIE   I know. I'm very sorry, but I introduced it.

Barry Humphries played, too. But he didn't know what to wear. As he was in a show at the time, he found an old hamper containing costumes from a musical called *Hit the Deck*, which was about the American Navy. So he dressed in white bellbottoms, and a seaman's vest and a rather old green cap. Unfortunately he went to the wrong ground, where they were actually playing a third grade match, and there were these rather butch Australians all sitting there with baggy green caps and pads on. Suddenly, in wafts Barry Humphries in his bellbottoms and his vest, saying, 'Sorry I'm late.' We heard the explosion from where we were . . . four grounds away.

BRIAN   Did you watch any serious cricket in Australia?

WILLIE   Yes, I was there for that wonderful morning at Sydney in 1966 when Barber and Boycott put on 234 for the first wicket. Boycott made 84, Barber 185 and John Edrich made a century as well. I had flown in that morning and I sat there in the sun wearing a little pork pie hat. Soon I was completely red and peeling from about halfway down the nose downwards. I wasn't bearded then so I was a sitting duck for the sun and I just sat and watched that magnificent batting.

BRIAN   And Barber's father was on the Hill watching him

make that century. And England won by an innings.

WILLIE   I'd never seen anything like it. I went into the bar there, and Australians have these tiny little drinks. They have huge hands and tiny drinks. So I bought a tray of twelve and went and sat down next to a man who had a face like a map of the Northern Territory, really creased up. 'Jeez,' he said, 'these Poms are showing us a thing or two,' – not recognising me as an Englishman – for which I was rather grateful at the time. I said, 'I cannot tell you, sir, how delighted I am to hear you say that. And I've only just flown in from the old country this morning.' He said, 'Effing Pom!' and stormed off. They don't lose gracefully.

BRIAN   Well, we won that match, and dear old David Brown took 5 for 63.

But well, Willie, you're still playing the game yourself. Do your legs begin to go when you bat yet?

WILLIE   They've gone permanently.

BRIAN   No, I mean after how many runs?

WILLIE   Well, I've given up twos. I only do ones and boundaries now, because I find 22 yards in full equipment is quite something.

BRIAN   Do you wear a sporting cap?

WILLIE   I've got an old red one that I had made by the Bert Oldfield shop in Sydney. I asked them to do me a good old baggy. It's not as baggy as they used to be, but it's still clearly an Australian shape. It's bright red and he didn't know what to put on the front of it so he put my initials, W.G.R., I'm very fond of it.

BRIAN   Thank you for being with us and for dressing so smartly.

WILLIE   For you, a tie Brian.

CHRISTOPHER LEE

THE SECOND TEST against Pakistan at Lord's in 1987 was one of the most frustrating of all the 256 Tests on which I have been lucky enough to commentate. In the whole five days there was no more than seven hours ten minutes of cricket. On the Saturday play did not start until 2.45 pm, but we were lucky to have one of the most talkative of all our guests in *Views from the Boundary* that day – Christopher Lee (complete with I Zingari tie). He has been described as tall, dark, and gruesome and, much to his displeasure, he is generally associated with horror films. In fact he only made fifteen of them, and, as he was swift to point out, he has made more films than any other British actor, and at the time of our conversation he had made no less than 162.

He used to play for Trevor Howard's Bowler Hat Club, and during his film making in Hollywood he also knew all the cricketing actors who played for Sir Aubrey Smith, such as David Niven, Nigel Bruce, Ronald Colman, Errol Flynn and Boris Karloff. Some people may not know that

Sir Aubrey – or 'Round the Corner Smith' as he was called – had the unusual record of being Captain of England in the only Test in which he ever played.

In addition to his love, and deep knowledge of cricket, Christopher has obviously got the golf bug. I was amazed to hear him claim that he has played with *all* the great golfers in the world, except Ben Hogan, and that at one time he had been scratch, even playing twice in the Amateur Championship. A versatile and very confident chap.

LORD'S, 20 JUNE 1987

CHRISTOPHER LEE   I started to learn cricket at my prep school, which was Somerfield's in Oxford. The bursar there was an extremely good bowler, but unfortunately he had a rather strange action, which – as one does at a very early age – I proceeded to copy. It's an action which was shared by Mike Procter and Max Walker, in other words it was rather like a windmill and I bowled off the wrong foot, swinging my arms over twice. I'm six foot four, so when I got going – and I did open the bowling; at public school as well on other occasions – if I kept any kind of length they used to come up fairly high off the pitch. I was fairly quick.

BRIAN JOHNSTON   You played for Wellington?

CHRISTOPHER   I did on occasions yes, and the highest score I ever got in my life was while I was at Wellington, but not playing for the College. I had a hundred and forty-nine not out. I came into the pavilion and burst into tears, because I didn't make a hundred and fifty.

BRIAN   And did you keep it up after school?

CHRISTOPHER   No, there was a little thing called World War Two, which inconveniently intervened in 1939. I'd just left school about a year before. I was what was called in those days, I suppose, a promising cricketer. I went in about four or five and fancied myself a lot, of course. Everybody used to say, 'What marvellous style,' when they saw me in the nets. 'Superb elegance of strokeplay.' It was very different when I got out into the middle. I was so concerned about making those magnificent looking shots, that I seldom scored enough runs.

BRIAN   And the RAF. You couldn't fit in a plane; you're too big.

CHRISTOPHER   Oh, I have been known to do that. Actually my cricketing career did continue during the war to a very minor degree. In fact I suppose the greatest moment of my whole life in the game of cricket was when my squadron – 260 Squadron in the Desert Air Force – had a game of cricket against one of the other squadrons, played on a rather bizarre pitch in the desert which had been flattened and rolled and had some matting put down. I took nine wickets. I didn't know what the ball was going to do any more than anybody else.

After the war I still played until 1950, when I virtually stopped. Of course I've never given up my love for the game and I watch it as often as I can, all over the world.

BRIAN   So, what about watching? Go right back to your first big match. Do you remember the first one you saw?

CHRISTOPHER   I think I can. It's very difficult, because it's at least fifty-five years ago. It was while I was at my prep school, and we watched a match played at Oxford, and I'm absolutely certain that Jack Hobbs was batting. It might have been Surrey against Oxford. And I certainly remember the pre-war Australian teams vividly. I remember Bradman as if he was walking out in front of me now. The thing I remember about him was the first time I ever saw him hit the ball, and that was his famous pull shot to the boundary from outside the off stump. I'd never seen a shot played like that. When I attempted it, I was sternly ordered by the games master not to try such rubbish, but to keep a straight bat.

BRIAN The other great batsman of that era that I was lucky enough to see was Wally Hammond. Did you see him?

CHRISTOPHER Oh yes, many times. I met him several times. Actually, I had a very dear friend, Bev Lyon, who was captain of Gloucestershire and of course he and Hammond used to play together. He told me a story once about the Gloucestershire scorecard. Frequently, when Charlie Parker was bowling, the scorecard would read 'Caught Lyon bowled Parker' many many times, because Bev used to field at second slip and Wally Hammond at first, and everyone who knows anything about cricket knows that Wally Hammond was one of the greatest slip fielders of all time. He was so fast that he took the ball and literally flicked it out of the back of his hand to Bev, who threw it up in the air. And it always went down as 'Caught Lyon bowled Parker'.

But my cricketing career came to an end really with the outbreak of war. Then I tried to take it up again, but only at weekends for fun after the war from 1946 onwards. I played in a marvellous place at Birkenhead, I remember – the Bowler Hat Club. I played for a team that Trevor Howard got together, all stage and screen people, against a Lancashire team. Ken Cranston was the captain and Jack Ikin was playing. I'll never forget the expression on

Trevor's face when I said boldly, 'I'll open the bowling,' and charged towards the crease with this rather strange bowling action. As my first arm went over I caught my hand on my right hip, and as my second arm went over there was nothing in my hand, and the batsman looked wildly round. Just a twirling arm. He didn't know what had happened to the ball. Nor did anybody until it was retrieved from the boundary behind me. It was a moment of great shame.

BRIAN   That would have been a dead ball, I suppose.

CHRISTOPHER   Trevor's face would have preferred a dead bowler.

BRIAN   Trevor used to play a bit for me. He was a jolly good cricketer.

CHRISTOPHER   Oh, yes and of course fanatically involved in the game.

BRIAN   And he had the famous clause in his contract that said he wouldn't film during Test Matches.

CHRISTOPHER   And there was, I believe, a similar clause in the contract of Boris Karloff, who was a tremendously keen cricketer, and indeed in Aubrey Smith's contract, too. There's a marvellous story about Aubrey Smith. He was apparently sitting here at Lord's, and watching some game going on and predictably snorting through his moustache saying, 'Good God, take him off. What a player!' The usual sort of remarks. He was then at the height of his fame as an actor and had been knighted, and was in every British film you could think of, or on any British subject made in Hollywood in those days. Everybody in the world knew him. Apparently two rather elderly members had been listening to this tirade going on and were getting a little disgruntled about it. One of them finally turned to the other and said, 'Who's that fellow over there making all that noise?' And the other one looked over and said, 'Oh, yes. That's a fellow called Smith. Used to play for Sussex.'

BRIAN   And Boris Karloff used to be a regular at the Oval. He was a member of Surrey, wasn't he?

CHRISTOPHER   And he also used to come here to Lord's a lot too. In fact I've watched matches with him here. He played for Uppingham when he was at school there.

BRIAN   Just remind us what his real name was.

CHRISTOPHER   William Henry Pratt.

BRIAN   Very advisable to change that.

CHRISTOPHER   Well, I suppose so. I never found out where the Karloff came from. Boris always said it was in the family somewhere. I remember asking his widow, Evie, 'Were you Boris's fifth wife?' And she said, 'As far as I know.' Because he was certainly married five times and possibly more, but a cloud of mystery hangs over that.

BRIAN   Sticking to Hollywood. You lived there for ten years. Any cricket going on nowadays?

CHRISTOPHER   Oh, yes, quite a bit. You see there are a lot of West Indians there, quite a lot of Pakistanis and people from countries that play cricket, like Fiji and various other places in the Pacific. There are quite a lot of teams out there and they play regularly on Saturdays and Sundays. I had a rather incredible experience really, because I hadn't played for well over thirty years, and Norman Gifford brought a team out, and I found myself playing on matting in the Rose Bowl at Pasadena. It's normally used for American Football, but it was a wonderful experience for me to be out there again with a bat in my hands. The years rolled back, up to a point. And the team was a remarkable one, because apart from Gifford himself, there was Graham Gooch, Glenn Turner, David Gower, Ian Botham and Geoff Miller. It was great fun because they kept on bowling me long hops.

BRIAN So you were among the runs that day were you?
CHRISTOPHER Yes, I made a few runs, believe it or not.
BRIAN But when Aubrey Smith was there, was there a club? What sort of ground did they have?
CHRISTOPHER They played on a ground in a place called Griffith Park, which still exists. But I don't think there's a cricket pitch there any more. I don't think they had any specific name as a team, but of course he was the captain and a very unforgiving one, too. David Niven, Basil Rathbone and Nigel Bruce played. I remember Boris used to tell very funny stories about these matches, because Aubrey Smith was a great dictator, and if you didn't make some runs or hold a few catches you were shamed almost for ever. In fact his house at the top of Coldwater Canyon had an exact replica of Father Time on the roof as a weathervane. He used to fly the MCC flag too.
BRIAN Back here, now, do you ever watch any cricket?
CHRISTOPHER I always try and come to Lord's for a Test, and if possible, on a Saturday or during the week if I'm free. Otherwise, I must admit I watch on television, and this is where the game has changed to such an immense

degree since the days when I first started watching it there at the ground. There are great improvements. You can see things in close-up. You can see the way the ball moves, both in the air and off the ground. You can see the batsman's footwork much more clearly. You can certainly see, in the replays, how somebody got out and what the ball did, which you could never do in those days. I think it's a great blessing to millions of people, who would otherwise never be able to watch cricket at all.

BRIAN   I think you and I were lucky to see some of the great players; the Hendrens and the Hobbs and the Woolleys. But maybe in ten years' time people will say, 'Wasn't it great, we saw Botham.'

CHRISTOPHER   I was lucky enough to see the man, who to my way of thinking was undoubtedly the greatest fast bowler, Harold Larwood. Lindwall would certainly be in second place, but Larwood was a phenomenal bowler. I've never seen anything to better the run-up, the action, the pace, or the accuracy. I think the best off spinner I ever saw was probably Tayfield.

BRIAN   He was very very accurate. Didn't spin it a lot, but difficult to get away.

I remember seeing Denis Compton play him, when Denis was on his best form, and he just hit it into the off field. He had a big off field, and he used to bowl well outside the off stump, and Denis couldn't penetrate the field at all.

But let's just talk about the acting, for a moment. You have this reputation – did you go straight into the horror films?

CHRISTOPHER   Not at all.

BRIAN   Do you mind being associated with horror films?

CHRISTOPHER   Well, yes and no. Let's put it this way. I've done them, not as many as people think, and they were instrumental in my beginning an international career, so I can never turn my back on them. Not that I wish to.

I started as an actor in 1947. I'm six-foot four, and in the first ten years of my career I never got a job of any consequence because people said, 'He's much too tall. We can't have him towering over the leading men.' Even the so-called giants of six foot two and three felt smaller beside me. In actual fact that's nonsense really, because I've been in a lot of pictures, 162 to be precise . . .

BRIAN   That's a staggering number.

CHRISTOPHER   It's more than anybody alive today. British actor, anyway. And I've had many people all over the world come up to me and say, 'I didn't realise you were so tall.' So that blows that theory out of the window. I started in films in 1957, by doing the first film for Hammer, a horror movie called *The Curse of Frankenstein*.

BRIAN   What were you then? You were the creature, weren't you?

CHRISTOPHER   That's right.

BRIAN   But the Dracula business. How many Dracula films?

CHRISTOPHER   Six in fifteen years.

BRIAN   But you were killed by spears in the eyes or heart.

CHRISTOPHER   And I've still got the scars to prove it!

In fact there's a lot of misconception about this. Out of all those pictures that I've made, I've only made fifteen horror movies. I played Dracula six times, and I haven't made a picture of that kind since 1971.

BRIAN   Who was the most attractive actress you bit in the neck?

CHRISTOPHER   I can't remember actually doing that, although it might have looked as if I had. Oh, they were all quite attractive. I don't think I'd better single one out. If you ask me who was the greatest actress I've ever worked with, that's an easy one. Bette Davis, by a mile.

BRIAN   Your other thing was golf. What handicap did you get down to?

CHRISTOPHER   I got down to scratch.

BRIAN   So who was the best player you played with?

CHRISTOPHER   I was very lucky. After living for ten years in America I have played with just about all of them. The only one I haven't played with is Ben Hogan, which is impossible. You don't get a game with Ben Hogan. He plays with his friends at Shady Oaks.

I had an incredible experience once in a tournament as the only amateur. They played in threes – one amateur and two professionals – and they were playing for an awful lot of money. So, if you put it in the rough, they weren't going to come and help you look. The first day I played with Lee Trevino and Craig Stadler. The second day with Johnny Miller and Gary Player, the third day with Gerry Pate and Seve Ballesteros and the fourth day with Greg Norman and Jack Nicklaus.

BRIAN   These are some names you're dropping.

CHRISTOPHER   Well, I'm just casting them casually. But you can just imagine the state of near paralysis I got into with twenty thousand people on the course. Though I'd played in the English Amateur Championship a couple of times, I'd never played with people lining the course, from tee to green.

BRIAN   And you've played with Richie Benaud.

CHRISTOPHER   Yes. The first time I ever played with him was in one of those BBC pro-celebrity things. It was at Gleneagles, and we had Seve Ballasteros and Lee Trevino, and as we walked down the first fairway I said, 'We must try and enjoy this, mustn't we? Because it's pretty unnerving.' And Richie said, 'Unnerving? This is worse than going out to try and save the Ashes.'

MICHAEL PARKINSON

OUR GUEST AT THE Headingley Test of 1984 was that most Yorkshire of Yorkshiremen, Michael Parkinson. Born and bred in Barnsley it was his great ambition to play cricket for Yorkshire. His father actively encouraged and supported him. But it was not to be. Parky became a good club cricketer, and used to open the batting for Barnsley. He has played a lot of charity cricket and takes his bowling very seriously. Woebetide anyone who drops a catch off him!

I suppose that basically Parky is a writer who later switched to television as a reporter, presenter and finally as one of its best interviewers with his own show, *Parkinson.* Cricket has always been his first love but funnily enough he has never become a cricket writer. Films were his main subject as a journalist.

He has always been interested in people, and not surprisingly his hero is Len Hutton. But he also strongly supported and helped the two Bs – Boycott (Geoff) and Best (George). In fact add Barnsley, and he could be described as a 3B man.

HEADINGLEY, 4 JULY 1987

BRIAN JOHNSTON   You are someone who might be called football daft and cricket mad. Which takes precedence, cricket or football?

MICHAEL PARKINSON   Oh, cricket. Cricket's been my great passion. I've stopped being involved in football in any sense. I don't like the game; I don't like what I see. When I watched football it was a funny game, full of character and full of skill as well, and that seems to have disappeared. I think cricket still manages to retain its character and sense of fun. I still enjoy meeting cricketers. I still enjoy yarning with them. I love being at a cricket match. It's part of my soul, really.

BRIAN   Born in Barnsley?

MICHAEL   I was born in a pit village just outside, called Cudworth, and my father was captain of the local cricket team. Being a cricketer in our family was obligatory. If you didn't play cricket you were banished. So I got my love of cricket from my father. He bought me my first cricket bat when I was four. He was a fanatical Yorkshire supporter, and I remember the very first game he took me to when I was about five, and I went to Bramall Lane and I sat on those cold steps in the football stand there, and it remains one of my favourite grounds. It's sad the stand has gone now.

BRIAN   It was a ground full of tremendous character.

MICHAEL   I played and I watched my father play through the war. I wanted to be a professional cricketer. That was my great ambition, and my father shared this ambition for me. He wanted me to play for Yorkshire and I went to the Yorkshire nets and wasn't good enough. I remember one or two people who were there with me, like Close and Illingworth, people like that. It was a fair team they had. And I always remember my father's remark – one of those occasions when you get a bit above yourself.

I got a job at the *Manchester Guardian* when I was about twenty-one, against all the odds. I came back across the Pennines that night and my father, being a miner and on day shift, was in bed and my mother was too, and I woke them up at about one in the morning because I was absolutely overjoyed, and I said, 'I got the job on the *Guardian*.' And my mother said, 'Well done, son, very well done.' My dad turned over and said, 'Well done lad, but it's not like playing cricket for Yorkshire, is it?'

BRIAN   How right he was. Do you have any memories of those pre-war Yorkshire players?

MICHAEL   No, I haven't. My earliest impression of a Yorkshire cricketer was pre-eminently Len Hutton, who was my great hero and still is. I still think he's the best opening batsman I've ever seen.

BRIAN   I was lucky to see him before the war. I don't know what difference the arm he damaged made to him.

MICHAEL   But it's interesting to speculate what he might have done in the intervening years. And I still think he's the benchmark of all opening bats.

BRIAN   A wonderful character, too. He's enigmatic. He looks at you and winks and whispers something and says, 'You know what I mean'.

MICHAEL   I heard a story about when he was on the selection committee, and Alec Bedser was chairman, and he had been at three meetings and hadn't said a word, and England weren't doing very well. And at the fourth meeting Alec said, 'Len, you've not said anything at all.' And Len said, 'Have you ever seen Fred Astaire and Ginger Rogers dance?' And what he was trying to say in that elliptical way of his was that footwork was what it was all about.

I also used to feel very sorry for young Richard (Hutton) who I thought was a very good player. I remember once at Bradford he played on a bad track there and scored a good thirty odd and he came into the pavilion and I was sitting there in the members' enclosure. And one daft guy stood up and said to him, 'Tha'll never be as good as thee dad.' And a guy sitting next to him said, 'Who was?'

BRIAN Can we go back to when you came to the nets here. Would Mitchell have been here coaching?

MICHAEL 'Ticker' Mitchell was here, yes. Maurice Leyland was here. Mitchell I remember was fearsome. Used to shout at you and I used to quake.

BRIAN Were they kind coaches, or cruel to be kind?

MICHAEL They were cruel to be kind. The thing about Yorkshire then was that the standard was so incredibly high. They could afford to be ruthless. I just knew that I wasn't good enough for that lot at all. I wasn't within measuring distance of the others.

BRIAN When I've seen you play over recent years, a brisk medium I would call you. Were you ever faster than that?

MICHAEL No, I wasn't. I actually wanted to be a batsman. I wanted to be Len Hutton, of course. So I concentrated on batting. I didn't bowl till later in my life. I played for Barnsley. I actually opened with Dickie Bird. I am immortalised in Geoffrey Boycott's autobiography. He recalls that I caused him to drop down the order from one to five, which he didn't like. I got fifty and next week in the first team I got a century and my children have been made to read it, so they know I'm not entirely a silly old man.

BRIAN   What was your best opening partnership with Dickie Bird?

MICHAEL   We put on two hundred and ten against Harrogate once. I got a century, and I ran him out when he was ninety-eight, and I got the collection and Dickie didn't.

BRIAN   Was he as nervous out there playing as he is before going out to umpire?

MICHAEL   He's not changed at all. He got four ducks on the trot once and so he dropped down the order. He got three first balls in that. I got out early in the next game, so I was watching him. He was going in number five, and he chewed through a pair of batting gloves, so when he went out he had open-ended gloves. He once sold all his gear, and we sold it back to him the next week at a vast profit. I played here (at Headingley) for Barnsley against Leeds in the Yorkshire League. The opening batsmen for Leeds were Arthur Clues (the old Australian rugby league player), a tremendous hitter of the ball, and Billy Sutcliffe, who was a very fine player. And they scored, I think it was two hundred and forty without loss, and every single run went past me at extra cover and rolled to the feet of the one spectator there, and he never moved. About the twentieth time I ran down there I said, 'Tha might throw it back.' He said, 'Nay, lad. I've coom here to see thee laik.'

BRIAN   So when did you give up any hope of being a first class cricketer?

MICHAEL   When I was in the army I played a lot of army cricket. I was down in Southern Command and I was playing for a team called the Moonrakers, who were a wonderful drinking side – and quite good at cricket actually – and one Sunday I was playing against a Hampshire side skippered by a man called Arthur Holt (Hampshire coach). I scored a lot of runs that day and soon they invited me along to the Hampshire nets, and I played for Hampshire Club and Ground on four or five occasions. Then they invited me to go on the second team tour, starting at Bristol and ending up in Kent. I went home on leave to get myself together, and then the War Office intervened and I went to Suez instead. When I came back I went to them having decided in that intervening period that it was a nice thought, but it didn't actually work out and I would not have made a good county player at all.

BRIAN   But Parky, a Yorkshireman playing for Hampshire!

MICHAEL   My father did not approve. I think that was the clinching argument. I couldn't tell him. But that was the end of it. I just concentrated on journalism.

BRIAN   But Captain Parky being called to Suez!

MICHAEL   I was Second Lieutenant Parky at the time. I was in Public Relations. I was in charge of the world's press. A man called Robin Essler, who later became editor of the *Sunday Express*, and myself were appointed to the field rank of captain, and we became the two youngest and silliest captains in the British Army. It was great fun. I met a lot of Fleet Street people out there who later I worked with.

BRIAN   So you became a journalist. What did you want to write about?

MICHAEL   I wanted to write about sport, really. But somehow I never did. It wasn't until much later in my career that I started to work for the *Sunday Times*, on a casual basis, writing that sports column which lasted for about fifteen years.

BRIAN   If they'd said, 'Would you be our *Sunday Times* cricket correspondent?', would you have accepted?

MICHAEL   I would have done fifteen years ago,

absolutely. But what happened was that television had intervened and I'd pursued a career in that and rather neglected the journalism. So the journalism I did so was on a very casual freelance basis, I suppose. Sometimes I look back and I regret that decision. Because, although financially it's been much better for me, I do envy you people who cover sport for a living, I really do. I think it's the greatest job in the world.

BRIAN   We're very, very lucky. You're also lucky that you get to go to Australia.

MICHAEL   And I enjoy that very much indeed. Australia's now a very important part of my life, and I settled in there very very easily. I think there's a kind of kinship between North country English and the Australians.

BRIAN   I'm surprised you haven't done any cricket commentary.

MICHAEL   I tried it for Yorkshire Television and Granada

and I'm very bad at it. I think it's a specific gift.

BRIAN   I'll tell you the secret of it. It's practice.

You're a great hero worshipper. I would have thought probably George Best was the chap you admired most of all.

MICHAEL   Well, I think George is the best footballer I ever saw, without doubt. I liked him immensely as a friend and I think he was a fairly misunderstood young man. He also did some rather silly things. But I've always felt about George that of all the rogues I've known, he was the most pleasant. I think the saddest thing was going to see him in prison. The thing about George was that when he walked into a room you knew he was there. He had that quality. The first time I went into this room in Pentonville Prison I looked round and I couldn't find him. There was that uniformity. I mean that's what they do, they make everyone look alike. I cringe when I tell you the story and I think that's why I've never written it. It's much too personal and much too hurtful.

My other heroes – I love raffish characters. I love K.R. Miller, I loved the way he played the game. And a chivalrous man, too.

BRIAN   And a great contrast with someone you obviously admired and you've defended a lot, and that is Geoffrey Boycott. You couldn't have a bigger contrast than him and Miller.

MICHAEL   You mean the puritan and the cavalier? But I admire Geoffrey Boycott for lots of reasons. I admire that determination and application that made him from an ordinary player into a very great player. I saw him at Barnsley when he came at fifteen and you would not have picked him then. With the old National Health specs taped to the back of his head. But he improved and improved. I remember one day we played at Scarborough and an old Yorkshire bowler called Bill Foord – you might remember him, medium-pacer – was there. It was a wet day and there was a pile of sawdust at the back, and Geoffrey got on the back foot – he was about sixteen – and he clobbered this guy straight back past him. It went through the sawdust for four. And Foord said to me, 'What's his name?' And I said, 'Boycott.' He said, 'I'll remember that.' And that was the start. That was Geoffrey coming up. He couldn't field, but you can learn to be a fielder.

BRIAN   And he became a marvellous thrower of the ball, from long leg or third man, straight into the gloves always.

MICHAEL   You see, I just admire that dedication. David Bairstow once said to me, 'You know, if the players would stop looking for his bad points and learn from his good points, they'd learn an awful lot about this game of cricket.'

BRIAN   You mentioned that drive back past the bowler. We didn't see a lot of that.

MICHAEL   I think Geoffrey became obsessed with the notion of staying there and of building a personal score, and in one way I understand why he did that. In another sense it was something of a denial of a very fine player. We all talk of his innings at Lord's *(146 in the 1965 Gillette Cup Final)*. I think this self-denial crept into his soul and was corrosive, but I still am a great admirer of Boycott, and if I had to pick a team to play for my life, he'd open for me.

BARRY JOHN

FOR CERTAIN 1987 was a Royal year for us. At Lord's we had a Royal Duke, the Duke of Edinburgh, and at Edgbaston a King, King John of Wales, alias the legendary rugby international Barry John.

In Wales he is thought of as the greatest fly half the rugby world has ever known, better even than Cliff Morgan. They had much in common, especially that indefinable skill of elusiveness. They could both glide their way through the opposition with a feint, or a side-step, which made it so difficult to lay a hand on them. You will see how generous a person he is when he lavishes praise on his partner, at scrum half in all but two of his internationals, Gareth Edwards. On top of his skill as a runner, orchestrator and perfect distributor of passes, Barry was also a superb place-kicker, and actually scored a record 180 points on the British Lions tour of 1971.

Since boyhood he had always followed and played cricket, and is a loyal supporter of Glamorgan. He really seemed to enjoy being with us in the commentary box.

EDGBASTON, 25 JULY 1987

BARRY JOHN   It's a great pleasure to be here. The radio in the car is always tuned in to Johnston and Co. And I'm a crawler, as well.

BRIAN JOHNSTON   You are, an absolute creep. I'm glad to see you're wearing the Primary Club tie. Can you remember when you qualified for that?

BARRY   Many years ago I was trying to impress my girlfriend – now my wife – and we went to a lovely place called Llangadog, which is in North Carmarthenshire. We'd beaten Llangadog twice, in fact we had to play them a lot of times, as there were only three teams in the league. And it was a lovely little common, and the place was plastered with sheep and a little river, and all the rest of it. And this bloke we hadn't seen in the previous games, a long dangling sort of Bob Willis type, he was a student and I thought he was full of wind and nothing else as he charged up. Nought point eight seconds later I joined the Primary Club. Everything went flying.

BRIAN   So how good a cricketer were you?

BARRY   I missed out a bit because of rugby tours. I used to play for a village called Cowbridge, in Tony Lewis country. I used to be the standard six or seven bat and third change bowler. Unfortunately we landed up with two tremendous opening bats, and very fine opening bowlers, and if I'd gone to the pub for a pint, no one would have noticed.

BRIAN   Tony tells me you nearly ruined a charity match.

He wanted the other side to make some runs, because someone had taken a few too many wickets, so he said, 'Come on and bowl Barry,' and you promptly took three wickets in one over.

BARRY   Well, yes, but I didn't quite qualify for the hattrick. I didn't bowl well. I think they just looked at the rugby player on the other side and they thought, 'Crikey, he must be good'.

BRIAN   Off your shortened run, was it?

BARRY   It had to be. The garden was nearby. But it is a fact that in one game I mesmerised them with some superb Abdul bowling, and after two overs I had one for three. Then one guy came in and I realised he couldn't care a damn and I finished off with five overs, one for sixty-three.

BRIAN   Have you got some Glamorgan heroes?

BARRY   I think of the 1969 boys (*Glamorgan's County Championship-winning side. Ed.*). They were obviously a very fine team.

BRIAN   And the old Wooller side of 1948.

BARRY   Well, being born in 1945 . . . give me a crack, will you? But obviously Tony Lewis, what he's done for Glamorgan has been magnificent, not only by example on the field, but what he's done off the field and the way he's gone about the game itself.

BRIAN   Are they keen on cricket in Wales, or is it secondary to the rugby?

BARRY   Of course, rugby is number one and top of the pops. You look at cricket in a different sort of way. It's something the rugby boys play to keep fit. Phil Bennett is a tremendous cricketer. He loves it. After the 1977 Lions tour, which had been a very muddy tour, he said that once he was at the bottom of a ruck and just felt like saying, 'What am I doing here? I could be opening the bowling at home, nice and gently for Felinfoel.'

BRIAN   Now, let's talk a little bit about rugby. First of all, this thing of 'King John'. Was it embarrassing to you? You were adulated, weren't you?

BARRY   Well, I've never taken any notice of the thing. If people say it, so be it. When people say, when you sign a couple of autographs, funnily enough one or two do still ask, 'Put in King John.' I say, 'Never.' The day you do that, that's the day you believe in it. So I've never done that and I won't.

BRIAN   But you must have read these things in the papers. Didn't they say, after the 1971 tour, that you wouldn't be flying back with the rest of the team, you'd be walking back across the ocean?

BARRY   But I missed my step. No, as far as I'm concerned, if people want to be complimentary and say nice things, then so be it. But it goes in one ear and out of the other.

BRIAN   But you got out of it a bit early, in 1972 at twenty-seven, that's young. Twenty-five caps.

BARRY   You've done your homework. Yes, by any stand-ards that's young, and I think I'm right in saying Cliff Morgan was the same age. But the circumstances were that I wasn't enjoying my life, and although that wasn't because of the rugby itself, it was caused by my playing rugby. The nicest part of it though was to stand in the middle of the field, in front of seventy or eighty thousand, and no one would come up and pester you.

BRIAN   And you play tennis, I know. So you're into all games, are you? Golf?

BARRY   Oh, yes. I'm a left-hander at golf, but really Gareth Edwards is the one. He's the only guy whose mantelpiece is reinforced. I'm very much a social golfer. When Peter Walker's running out of golf balls, he gives me a ring.

People talk about this ultra-competitive streak. But you don't need the nastiness. You know what you've got to do, even at the highest level. If you prepare yourself properly, mentally and physically, you know what's expected of you.

BRIAN I bet you do when you run out at Cardiff Arms Park with all those people watching you.

BARRY Oh, it's the most unbelievable feeling to run out there and when 'Land of My Fathers' starts, it's tremendous.

BRIAN Did you play your last international there?

BARRY Yes, against France in 1972.

BRIAN Take us through it. Did you score a brilliant, weaving try?

BARRY No, by that time I wasn't able to play the type of rugby I wanted to, because I think, the opposition showed too much respect. All I had to do was to catch and kick and take one or two players out of the game. When you've boys like Gareth (Edwards) on your inside, and Gerald Davies, J.P.R. (Williams) and John Dawes on the outside, it's like letting greyhounds off the leash.

BRIAN You're being modest and saying you passed it on and left it to them.

BARRY I think Bill Shankly once said to Steve Heighway, who wasn't happy on the wing and not seeing enough ball, 'You just stand on that corner flag and you take two of their fellows out of the game, and I'll double your wages. Forget about enjoying the game.'

BRIAN But they had to watch you because you were an elusive creature. They couldn't lay hands on you.

BARRY Obviously I'd be a hypocrite if I didn't accept that I was given a certain gift. I saw things very early. I knew where players were standing, even if a player was seventy yards away from the play. An inbuilt mechanism tells you

he's out of position.

BRIAN   That's very like Bradman. He said that he always looked before each ball where the fielders were on the off side and where they were on the leg, and he said, 'Right, if it comes on the off side, I'll hit it in that gap, and if it's on the leg in that gap.' He planned it all.

BARRY   It's a very fine line. When you beat people, others say later, 'They were close to you,' but they forget that at the moment we were closest we were going away from each other. A second later we were miles apart.

BRIAN   Did you learn this because you had a bit of a thrashing from the wing forwards when you started? Or not?

BARRY   Not really, no.

BRIAN   Did you have Gareth at scrum half for all the twenty-five games?

BARRY   No. The first scrum half I had was a guy called Alun Lewis from Abertillery, and the second was Billy Hullin of Cardiff. After that, when I clicked with Gareth, off we went on twenty-three straight games.

BRIAN   And the good long pass?

BARRY   Well, one of the reasons I retired was when he cut it down to thirty yards, I thought that's it.

BRIAN   When you played your last game, is it true that you said, 'I will score a try in the last minute in the corner'?

BARRY   Well, the game was between the great Carwyn James' fifteen, and my side. And it was played to raise funds for the Welsh League of Youth. And no one knew I was going to finish that day except Gareth and Gerald Davies, and we were like the three musketeers, have boots, will travel. We had a great time. So obviously I did confide in them. And I did say I wouldn't mind going out on a little note.

BRIAN   So you scored a try in the corner, did you?

BARRY   Well, ten yards to the left.

BRIAN   And what about the great 1971 Lions tour to New Zealand?

BARRY   It was like being on a magic carpet. We won all the provincial games for the first time ever, and we were leading two-one in the Test series. Before going out Doug Smith, the manager, prophesied that we'd win two-one, with one draw. The last one was a draw, fourteen-all in Auckland.

I was listening to Nick Faldo talking the other day and he made a point I agree with about something sinking in. Because when you've put something on a pedestal like that and you do eventually crack it, in fact there's a little disappointment about it. Now what's after this?

BRIAN   You got a little matter of 180 points on that tour.

BARRY   Well, one kick went in off the upright.

BRIAN   Now, on a cricket tour they're playing most of the time. In rugby you're playing eighty minutes twice a week.

BARRY   The big games are on Saturday. Normally on Lions tours you get the T and Ws and the Saturday team. People don't like this, but the T and Ws means the Tuesday and Wednesday team, and the Saturday team is basically the first team. Under that system at least people know where they are. There's a lot of travel, and you train every day, well the others did. I didn't train that much, to be honest. I carried a soccer ball with me. You can get fed up with rugby all the time.

BRIAN   Tours were fun in addition to playing, were they?

BARRY   Oh, it was a pleasure. As long as the boys enjoy it they'll overcome other things, but unfortunately I don't seem to smell the same type of feeling and enjoyment.

BRIAN   In cricket these days there is dissent being shown with umpires' decisions. You don't have that in rugby.

BARRY   No, you utter a few things and hopefully the referees take it in the right spirit. If you call him a right so-and-so, fair enough, he probably knows it, anyway. But cricket and tennis were always the games that represented fair play. Unfortunately now, with your McEnroes . . . I'd like to see him playing rugby, one game and I think the boys would have sorted him out.

BRIAN   Were you a great one for selling dummies, which I used to like to do?

BARRY   Yes, I remember talking to people about your dummies. They were quite famous, weren't they? Tell me about your favourite dummy.

BRIAN   No, but I'll tell you about a try I did once score in a macintosh. Someone pulled off my shorts and someone else said, 'You'd better wear this macintosh to hide your confusion.' So I joined in like that. I saw the ball coming down the line, and the referee was laughing so much that he couldn't whistle, so I scored under the posts.

But after any of your weaving runs, when you've touched down under the posts, has anyone ever come up and kissed you?

BARRY   No, never, and thank goodness for that.

BRIAN   And yet, if you were out there this afternoon with your famous leg breaks and you took a wicket, they'd all come up and kiss you.

BARRY   I'd probably bowl wides then.

WILLIAM FRANKLYN

AT THE OVAL TEST in 1987 I got the answer to a question which I had always wanted to ask. Was it William Franklyn himself who actually said 'Sccccchhhh', in that well-known tv advertisement for a certain drink? The answer was no he didn't, someone else was paid to do it.

Until I first met him I had always thought that Bill was an Australian. There was a good reason for this. He was brought up there as a small boy and educated at Haileybury in Melbourne, but he was born in England.

Bill is certainly the keenest of all the actor cricketers. He keeps very fit, runs his own team – The Sargent men – in aid of the Malcolm Sargent Cancer Fund, and has regular nets throughout the winter. As a young man he bowled fast-medium, but has now reverted to fairly high-flighted leg-breaks. In addition to his own side, he plays for the Lord's Taverners, the *Stage* and in fact for anyone who will ask him. When he is not playing he watches a lot of cricket, a pastime especially suited to actors, even when acting in a play.

THE OVAL, 8 AUGUST 1987

BRIAN JOHNSTON   A lot of people think you're Australian.

WILLIAM FRANKLYN   No, it just happens that my father went out there in 1926 to do musical comedy. He went out on an eighteen-month contract. He'd just played a part in London and, as often happens with a success, people flock round. Well, in those days before television, an Australian flocked round him and said, 'Would you like to go to Australia for eighteen months?' And the money seemed to be very good and he suddenly thought of the sun – the actual S-U-N, as well as the S-O-N – he thought it would be good for me too.

So off we pushed to Australia, and we stayed ten years. So I had my formative years out there, and I had to have a little bit of coaching now and again, because I had the patois naturally. They knew that when I came back to England I would be a real outsider, because in those days if you spoke like that in England – whereas today we enjoy it – then you were a bit odd.

BRIAN   So how much cricket did you see there, and how many cricketers did you get to meet?

WILLIAM   In those days the actors in Australia always played the current Australian Test side, that was a stand-ard thing, at Rushcutter's Bay (in Sydney). It's a very pretty, charming little ground. And that's where it all started, I suppose. My old man had, from the First World War, no knuckle to the third finger of his left hand. He was a left arm spin bowler and that finger used to lie indolently and incapable under the ball. And he actually caught and bowled Don Bradman in this match and they became very good friends.

I remember once we came along to this ground (the Oval) and watched Len Hutton make his 364 (in 1938). We sat all through that entire match actually down at the front. There were no boards up there; we sat on the grass at the edge. And Don Bradman actually bowled in that 903 for 7, until he was taken off with a 'crook ankle'. My old man went to see him in the hotel, and spent two or three days with him. He wanted somebody to take his mind away from cricket, because obviously what had happened was very disappointing.

BRIAN   Was your father a funny man in himself?

WILLIAM   He could be. He had great passions, for animals, for cricket, for Churchill and for the Royal Family. He loved his work enormously. He loved his cricket enormously too, and I don't necessarily say that he infected me, but I think genetically we do pass something on to each other. We pass on one of the lucky things – it's not something I could ever claim as a talent – if you have timing in any way, whether it be in sport, in writing or anything, I think he passed that on to me. But that was only luck, I think.

BRIAN   Were you coached in cricket?

WILLIAM   Oh, avidly. At school in Australia you had the Under Nines, the Under Elevens, the Under Thirteens, the Under Fifteens. So constantly you had the competitive thing of trying to move up into the next team.

My first real visual memory of cricket was sitting on the Hill in Sydney and watching Stan McCabe get 187.

BRIAN   You're talking of the Bodyline series. Did that impress you at the time?

WILLIAM   In bodyline the ball didn't get up compared

with what we've seen in the last few years. I think in those days the young Australian media had a rather fertile imagination, and I think that what today would have been regarded as fairly innocuous, was given some rather hysterical attention.

When the Australians made a film on the Bodyline series, I think my favourite moment was when somebody at deep square leg took a catch and yelled, 'How's that!' I think that was a moment that all cricketers must have loved.

BRIAN   They didn't get everything right. Lord Harris was a feature of the film, and the poor chap died in March 1932, before the tour started.

WILLIAM   And I don't think the wicket keeper stood up to Harold Larwood.

BRIAN   If he did, he never did again.

So let's come to 1938. You saw every day of Hutton's match. Was there a great sense of excitement when he was coming up to his record?

WILLIAM   Oh, yes. Of course you got the wit of Surrey. The Oval's always had its own wit. But you never got any kind of excessive noise or barracking. Most of them were aficionados of the game and they were watching with great intensity and they would comment to each other, some of them very wry, very witty, and always studied. They were academics, really, at every level.

BRIAN   Now, what about your own cricket. We've played cricket together. You were a fast-medium bowler. I gather you've slowed down a little now.

WILLIAM   Well, this year I hurt my arm in the nets early in the season just before going in to bat one day. I put my arm up to fend one off my face instead of ducking, as I might have done a few years ago, and at that moment someone said, 'You're in.' So I went in, and I don't normally bat for an hour and a half, I get on with it. But I couldn't get on with it because of the pain in my arm. So I got a very slow and very boring twenty-three not out. Three days later my wife said, 'You're wincing quite a lot.' And I said, 'I think it's the muscle. It must have taken a bruising.' So I went and had it X-rayed and it was actually broken.

The long and the short of the story is that despite being in plaster, I still went on playing cricket. You don't give it up because of it. And I even bowl, it has made me take my left shoulder higher, and I've started to get my outswinger back at a slower speed, but it's swinging better. And as a chum said the other day, 'You ought to break your arm at the beginning of every season.' And I said, 'I think I'll do it in the winter. Then I can actually enjoy the season.'

BRIAN   So what about the spin?

WILLIAM   Well, I tried leggies, though that takes me back a long way. I started leg breaks – very inadequate leg breaks – some time ago. Do you remember Arthur Mailey the great Australian player, who became a cricket writer? Well, Arthur Mailey was a friend of my father's, and on one of his last visits to England, which must have been in the Sixties, I said, 'The one thing I've never been able to understand is the googly.' We were in my parents' flat and there was no ball there, so he said, 'Have you got a cup, Mary?' And Mary went and duly got a cup, and he tried to show me how to bowl a googly with this cup. My father put cushions up against the wall so that he could actually do the action and let the cup go.

I'm afraid I never mastered the googly, because all I can think of is that wretched handle on the side, and as soon as I get the idea to bowl one I find I have seven fingers, all of which have become arthritic.

Now, I'm going to take you back a little further, to

Australia. My father loved golf, and he played with quite a lot of the Test players, including Herbert Sutcliffe, Patsy Hendren, Alan Kippax and Arthur Mailey. One time Dad drove down with them to La Perouse, which is near Botany Bay, and as they were driving there they saw some young kids playing cricket and Dad said, 'Look, just for fun, let's stop and have a game with them.' Herbert Sutcliffe took the bat and he held it rather clumsily, and this young tousle-haired Australian boy said, 'You're not holding it right, give it to me, I'll show you.' And this young boy showed Herbert Sutcliffe how to hold a bat.

Later on Dad said, 'You know that's Herbert Sutcliffe.' And he said, 'Yeah, and I'm Don Bradman.' And they will never know, unless they happen to be listening today, that they were with Alan Kippax, Arthur Mailey, Patsy Hendren and Herbert Sutcliffe.

BRIAN   So your dad kept company with the players?

WILLIAM   Well, in Australia it was a big thing. They're very similar professions. When I arrived here today the innings was just about to start, and to me that was just before the curtain went up. I could feel the tension in myself, that any actor might feel, when I saw Broad and Moxon coming out. I thought, 'They've got all this crowd here and there's a lot hanging on it. And you've got to go

143

out there and do something for them.'

BRIAN   Barry Richards was up here yesterday, and he said he regrets having got fed up with cricket, but performing before two men and a dog meant that he couldn't give of his best. And that's the same with actors.

WILLIAM   Exactly. Many years ago I played at Lord's against the Cross Arrows, and I remember E.W. Swanton bowled me over my left shoulder as I dropped onto one leg. And as I was playing this appalling shot, I looked at the twelve people in the Mound Stand, and I reflected that that was all the audience I deserved. But I can imagine it could be very lonely as a professional.

BRIAN   Jim Swanton's holy rollers, we used to call them. Though they didn't roll much.

Now, you're playing a lot for the Taverners, as well as having your own side.

WILLIAM   Yes, the Sargent Men, as we call them; for the Malcolm Sargent Cancer Fund for Children. Cricket, squash and football, until we all decided we were getting a little past that. We've been playing charity matches for about fifteen years. It was a very small charity when it began. The great thing about our side is that we don't have rigged matches, we actually play serious cricket, but with an enormous sense of humour. And you can imagine the chat that goes on. We don't actually stand in the field quietly. The slips are a raving madhouse of dialogue of all types, and that is part of the fun, and I think the people we go and play sometimes say, 'Will you come back and play us in a real game next year?' And from two or three fixtures, we've suddenly got ten or twelve.

BRIAN   Did you become an actor because of your father?

WILLIAM   I think it was all accidental actually. I wanted to be Sefton Delmer. Now, Sefton Delmer, for those who don't remember, was a foreign correspondent. I wanted to have a camera and a typewriter. It was a total fantasy, of course.

BRIAN   He always had scoops about Hitler, didn't he?

WILLIAM   It was like Walter Mitty. I wanted to be a fighter pilot and a submarine commander and a foreign correspondent and open for England. I couldn't do all those at the same time, although I reckon that C.B. Fry made a good stab at it. And I said this to Ray Smith of Essex, and he gave me what we might loosely – very loosely – call a trial for Essex. He said, 'You can play with the Essex side. We're playing Slough,' who at that time had got about four minor county players, and had done quite well for Buckinghamshire against the Australians that year. Anyway, Ray Smith gave me the new ball and said, 'You open the bowling.' And at one point I actually had 4 wickets for about 9 runs. I was very young. I went up to Ray and said, 'Do you think I ought to ease up a bit?' And he said, 'No,' and he left me on. I came off with 4 for 84 and he said, 'That's what the game is about.' It taught me a wonderful lesson.

BRIAN   Which do you prefer, television or the stage?

WILLIAM   It depends on the part, really. It's really like bowling if there's a bit of low cloud and it's swinging, or batting if it's a crisp day and the ball's coming on. Which is best? It's the same with an actor, I think. It's the parts. But I think the theatre does summon most of us back. That is the womb. That's the grass-roots of our business.

BRIAN   Anything brewing at the moment?

WILLIAM   Well, I was about to start rehearsing *Loot*, but that's been put off till the spring, and so I'm going to do rather more cricket nets this winter.

BRIAN   So next year Franklyn will be among the wickets early on. And don't ease off, will you, ever.

WILLIAM   I don't think I ever could. I am addicted.

HRH THE DUKE OF EDINBURGH

WE WERE VERY honoured that in MCC's Bicentenary year of 1987 the Duke of Edinburgh consented to be our guest in *Views from the Boundary* for the Bicentenary Match at Lord's. I say 'for' because for the first and only time so far, we made a recording of the conversation. The Bicentenary Match was in the third week of August which by Royal custom is holiday time at Balmoral Castle. So towards the end of July Peter Baxter and I went to Buckingham Palace to record HRH in his study in the north-east corner of the Palace. I admit that I was a bit apprehensive, though not about meeting the Duke whom I had met on a good many occasions, but for another reason entirely.

My first meeting with him had been at the Lord's Taverners' Ball at Grosvenor House in the early nineteen fifties. I ended up lying on the dance floor right in front of his table! It was during one of those 'events' which took place every year at the ball. This was an Olympic Games, in which the Lord's Taverners took on (and of course won – they always did) the Rest of the World. I represented the

Taverners in the three-legged race, and was the middle-
man between Macdonald Hobley and Peter Haigh. As we
were racing across the slippery floor we slid and fell.
Unfortunately, since my arms were round the shoulders
of my two partners, I was unable to break my fall, and I
landed on my left shoulder. I was in great pain, but of
course put on a brave smile in front of our twelfth man. It
was later diagnosed as a dislocated shoulder, not something I would recommend to anyone.

That was my first meeting with the Duke. Another occasion was the Queen's Jubilee in 1977, when Her Majesty
did a 'walkabout' from St Paul's to the Guildhall. For
some reason, which I have never discovered, I was
allowed to follow closely behind the Queen with a mobile
transmitter, describing the scene and asking the crowds
what the Queen had said to them when she stopped to
talk. Several years later, at a press reception aboard the
Royal yacht, the Queen told a BBC producer that she had
heard me asking my questions, and suddenly realised that
she must vary hers from the usual 'Where do you come
from?' or 'How long have you been here this morning?' All
this time the Duke was following a long way behind,
chatting up the crowds who were roaring with laughter.
As we approached the Guildhall he hurried forward to
join the Queen. I saw him coming up behind me and did
the unforgivable thing, I thrust my microphone in front of
him and asked whether he was enjoying himself. He
looked slightly taken aback at this breach of protocol, but
nevertheless smilingly shouted above the noise of the
cheering, 'I can't hear myself think!'

But the reason for my apprehension, on this particular
visit, was what had happened the last time I had been to
the Palace to interview the Duke for *Down Your Way*. We
were doing a programme on the National Playing Fields

Association of which he is the President.

We were shown into his study, and his private secretary asked me to sit on a sofa with my microphone. He then went to fetch the Duke, and placed him in an armchair on the opposite side of the large room. I had to explain rather nervously that we would have to sit a bit closer as we only had one microphone. So, muttering something about Auntie's ancient equipment, he came over and sat next to me. After that the interview went well, except that once again protocol was broken as our knees touched from time to time.

As a result of this incident for *Views from the Boundary* Peter Baxter made sure that we each had our individual lapel microphones, and so we were able to sit at a reasonable distance from each other, and prove that Auntie had become slap up to date!

LORD'S, 22 AUGUST 1987

BRIAN JOHNSTON   Your Royal Highness, it's very nice of you to join us on *Test Match Special*, and we're not known for our modesty, so can I start off by asking you how good a cricketer were you when you were a boy?

HIS ROYAL HIGHNESS   Well, I was never very good. I started at my prep school, Cheam, and then I had a bit of a break, because I went away to Germany for a year to school, and then came back again to Scotland and played there until I joined the Navy.

BRIAN   I rather cheated I'm afraid, because I found a

report of you at Cheam which said, 'An energetic all-rounder, highly unsympathetic to stonewalling.' A hard hitting batsman?

HRH   Well, I may have tried to hit it hard but I don't think I really succeeded all that often.

BRIAN   And what about Gordonstoun? Did they take cricket seriously there?

HRH   Well, fairly seriously, yes. But the only problem was that I was there right at the beginning, and we didn't have a ground or a pitch. We used to go to the public park at Elgin and play there. But it was quite fun. We played all sorts of people, like the Army at Fort George, and various schools.

BRIAN   And was there any cricket in the Navy?

HRH   Very little, because I joined in the summer of 1939 and so was rather pitchforked into the war, and there was really very little opportunity to play cricket. I did play once though, just after the war, in Malta, and I had one ghastly match in Akaba. That's not a place to play cricket in my opinion, and I know exactly what it feels like to run out of water in the desert. After I'd bowled three overs my tongue swelled up to such a degree that I couldn't breathe.

I had a short period after the war when I played at Windsor. Do you remember the cartoonist Jackie Broome?

BRIAN   Oh yes.

HRH   I remember one glorious occasion when I thought I'd bowl a googly. It came out of the back of my hand and when it hit the ground it actually used to go the wrong way, but this time it flew fairly high into the air and Jackie Broome saw this coming and ducked, whereupon it hit the wicket full toss. He then did a splendid cartoon of this ball arriving.

BRIAN   A thing like 'Spedigue's Dropper.'

HRH   That's right.

BRIAN   I'm told that you once took 1 for 12 against Hampshire.

HRH   George Newman organised a series of matches for the National Playing Fields Association. The first one was at Bournemouth, the first time I'd ever played on a good pitch. I rather enjoyed it, and of course playing with first-class cricketers. They had a marvellous way of organising the game.

BRIAN   They're pretty cunning, aren't they?

HRH   Yes. Everybody was allowed to get off the mark, but there came a moment when it was considered that they'd had enough. Things got quite serious then. John Reid played in that match, and I think he made the fastest fifty I think that anybody's ever made anywhere.

BRIAN   Not off your bowling though?

HRH   No, I think he was on my side. I thought I did rather well though, making 25 runs. And at Arundel one thing I do remember is that I had Tom Graveney caught at short leg, which of course caused enormous hilarity all round.

BRIAN   What about the great moment in 1950 when you were approached by Martin Boddey and Co. to become patron of the Lord's Taverners?

HRH   I said that 'patron' was a rather stuffy title for that sort of thing, so I suggested 'Twelfth Man'.

In the early days I suggested to them that rather than go through all the business of actually making the donations and finding things to give the money to, their best bet would be to give it to the National Playing Fields Association, but with certain conditions. They should put one of their members onto the committee, because all the contacts were already there and they could distribute the money much more cheaply. That started them off and they were very successful.

BRIAN   And now they raise a million pounds a year.

In 1949 you became President of the MCC. Was this unexpected?

HRH   Totally, yes. I didn't know much about it, but I took some soundings and people said, 'Yes, go ahead.' So I accepted.

It was quite interesting, because it was at a time when cricket fixtures were growing at a tremendous rate, and I could foresee that the demand on first-class cricketers' time would be so great that there would be no room for the amateur. I suggested then that they ought to have the county matches at the weekend, so that the amateurs could take part, and in midweek there should be a professional league with groups of counties. Now the whole thing's become professional and squeezed out the gifted amateur. Which is a pity.

BRIAN   Wasn't it rather awe-inspiring when you had your first meeting there with all those august members?

HRH   They're a very jolly lot, really. I've found the great thing in most sports is that provided you're interested in the sport, age or background make not the slightest difference. I was president of the International Equestrian Federation for years and I found exactly the same thing. If you've got an interest in the thing, people forget about everything else.

BRIAN   Then, unusually, you accepted to be MCC President for a second year in 1974.

HRH   Well, I was asked, and it seemed to me that it was something that would be quite amusing to have in the record books. Actually, I discovered that there was a much more sinister reason for my being asked again, and that was that the committee wanted to put up the subscriptions. So I walked into the Annual General Meeting to preside and was given the agenda which said that they'd proposed the increases in the subscription . . . and I suddenly realised why I'd been asked back again.

BRIAN   But surely no one dared to boo you.

HRH   Well, they did.

BRIAN   What about the role of the MCC today?

HRH   I think the idea that one club can be the central club in England, and also the governing body for the sport worldwide is nowadays very unreasonable. I think that the club has got the same responsibility that it always had, but inevitably it's got to share the responsibility for Test Matches and international cricket generally with a wider body. It's marvellous to say, 'Oh, this is the way it always used to be,' but the whole picture of cricket is different now. It isn't played the way it was forty years ago and it's not organised that way any more either. There's so much more of it and there's so much more international cricket to oversee.

BRIAN   What about the National Playing Fields Association? You're still very much involved as president of that.

HRH   We ran into difficulties over the charity law,

because as the NPFA is a charity, and originally helped out village clubs and anybody who wanted to play cricket, it is not allowed to give to an organisation that is not itself a charity. So now, the main emphasis is on children's playgrounds and the whole range of children's play, because funnily enough, it doesn't come under the Sports Council, and there is really no one who co-ordinates the whole spectrum of children's play. The situation in that area is a bit confused at the moment, but there's plenty for the NPFA to do.

Local authorities do, of course, help a great deal, but they vary from one place to another. And of course with the provision of playing fields and play space, you've also got to get at the planning authorities, the new towns' people and the development corporations who actually make provision for that space. We found that in the days of the new towns for instance we had the greatest difficulty in persuading them to leave room for playing fields.
BRIAN And they are being encroached on more and more, aren't they? That's rather serious.
HRH   That's another difficulty, you see, with the price of

land so high. A lot of companies with their own playing fields wanted to expand, so they expanded onto those playing fields. One of the things that we try very hard to do is to get employers in a town to gang together and provide playing fields on a community basis for everybody.

Now, of course, the difficulty is that even local authorities are beginning to get rid of playing fields because they want to earn some money. Play space has had a pretty rough time in the last few years.

BRIAN Do you regard team games and competitive games as important?

HRH Well I do, yes. The important thing about team games is that they're really part of social education, and it's the sort of education you don't get anywhere else. You learn to co-operate, you learn to sublimate your personality into the team, you have to learn to win, and I think that's very good for people. Team games are, in a sense, not over competitive unless you get into the professional end. In amateur sport, generally, people go and enjoy themselves. I go in for this carriage driving and it's great fun.

BRIAN Is it as dangerous as it looks? Have you been pulled off the box?

HRH Most people have turned over at some stage or another.

BRIAN You make it sound very casual.

HRH It's not as bad as that.

BRIAN It looks terrifying.

In contrast to all this, you have the Duke of Edinburgh Awards, which are very much for individuals, aren't they?

HRH That's the service section, which is individual, although you can do that through a group or an organisation. There's a skill section which you can do in a group, perhaps in amateur theatricals or something of that sort. But those two sections can be done individually. Then there's a physical recreation section which you can do individually or through team games, and then there's the expedition section where you have to go in a group of four, at least.

For a Gold Award one of the conditions is that you have to go away for a residential course for a weekend, and of course for many young people that's the first time they've ever been away from home. They have to mix with other people, so it's a genuine community activity.

BRIAN What made you start it?

HRH It's rather a long story, but I remember a similar thing being started by my headmaster at Gordonstoun, Kurt Hahn. And he came to me in about 1954 and said, 'My boy, I want you to start an award scheme.' And I said, 'Well, you get a group together and I'll come and chair it.' And he did.

The aim of the exercise was to provide an introduction to the sort of activities that adults found interesting and rewarding, which in most cases were not included in ordinary formal education. They were the sort of things which took place at boarding schools but not often in any other schools. It's now running in forty odd countries, I think.

BRIAN It's a very nice success story.

Can we just come back to cricket in this bicentenary year. Is there anything about modern cricket you'd like to see changed?

HRH No, I don't think so. I only wish that sometimes some of their trousers fitted a bit better.

BRIAN Well, sir, thank you very much.

I'm still going to maintain that you're the only chap who's been President of the MCC twice.

HRH Don't close the book yet, there may be a third time in another twenty-five years.

ROBERT POWELL

 I ONCE SAW A FILM starring George Arliss called *The Man Who Played God.* And at Lord's in 1988 I talked to the man who played Jesus Christ, Robert Powell. Now I don't know whether George Arliss ever played cricket. If he had, he would have been the only player ever to wear a monocle at the crease. But Robert both loves and plays cricket. He is a member of the MCC, lives in Highgate and watches quite a lot of cricket at Lord's. He plays for the Lord's Taverners, and by their standards bowls straighter than most.

In the acting profession, especially in television, there is always the danger of being typecast, and in spite of his Jesus Christ being a one-off part, there is still an aura of sanctity about Robert. He is a modest, very nice, friendly and normal person. But on first meeting him people tend to behave with exaggerated respect and politeness. Luckily he is an old friend of mine and there was no danger of me treating him other than as a very likeable cricket lover, smartly dressed with his MCC tie. I couldn't resist introducing him as 'a cricketer who occasionally acts!'

LORD'S, 18 JUNE 1988

BRIAN JOHNSTON   Robert, you look immaculately dressed today in your drill trousers and nice MCC tie, but it was in 1979 that you were elected the best-dressed man in Great Britain. What clothes did you wear to get that?

ROBERT POWELL   I don't know. I think it was people's perception of the parts I was playing then. I was playing rather dressy parts at the time; very period. In fact, I was pretty scruffy in those days. I never wore a tie, and, when this was revealed to the people who voted for me in 1979, it was received with deep shock.

BRIAN   Did you get a free suit or anything like that as a prize?

ROBERT   Well, yes I did.

BRIAN   Well, you haven't worn it today.

ROBERT   No, it's long since died.

BRIAN   Well let's get rid of one thing right at the start. You're not unknown as the chap who once played Jesus in *Jesus of Nazareth*. Is this an awful sort of weight on your shoulders?

ROBERT   Not really.

BRIAN   People treat you with great reverence don't they?

ROBERT   Well, I get a lot of jokes about it, but no, I don't mind. I'd be unhappy if people didn't remember it, and that would worry me more than people remembering it. I'm delighted really. I think in about forty or fifty years time I'd be quite happy if they said, 'the man who played Jesus' in my obituary.

BRIAN   I'm looking at your eyes behind these slightly tinted glasses. I'm told it was because of the look in your eyes that you were selected. Is that so?

ROBERT   I don't know. I would hate to think that was the only reason I was chosen.

BRIAN   I'm sure there were other parts of you just as good.

ROBERT   There still are other bits of me that are quite reasonable.

BRIAN   Come on, let's talk about cricket now.

ROBERT   Yes, please.

BRIAN   You're Lancashire born and bred. Where did you play? Where did you go to school?

ROBERT   Manchester Grammar School, and when I joined D.M. Green was school skipper. He went on to play for Lancashire and, I think, Gloucestershire.

BRIAN   Yes, and he now writes very well about cricket too. Very knowledgeable.

What did you aspire to do as a boy in cricket?

ROBERT   Bowler – absolutely. A lot of actors have role-models in life of people like Richardson and Gielgud and Olivier. My role-model in life has always been and will always be Brian Statham. I act as well, but Statham is the person I aspire to.

BRIAN   Do you bowl quite as straight as him?

ROBERT   My mother reminded me that when I was twelve or thirteen in Salford we had a long back garden, about 30 yards long in fact. And I stuck one stump in and had a six yard run-up, and used to bowl six cork balls at that stump hour after hour after hour. And the hedge behind the stump fielded for me.

I used to bowl quite straight, yes.

BRIAN   Was the stump fairly safe, or did you hit now and again?

ROBERT   I used to whack the stump. As a youngster I was not a bad sort of medium-pace bowler.

BRIAN   And you used to go along to Old Trafford and watch in those days?

ROBERT   Oh yes.

BRIAN   Who would have been going strong then?

ROBERT   Cyril Washbrook.

BRIAN   Wishy Washbrook. Marvellous cover point, and he used to cut the ball beautifully.

ROBERT   And obviously there was Brian Statham, who I saw at the Centenary Test dinner, which was marvellous, because I hadn't actually ever got his autograph, and I managed to get it there.

BRIAN   Lovely chap, isn't he? He was about the only fast bowler who used to talk to his feet. When he sat in the dressing-room he took his boots off and apologised to his feet for having put them through it.

Are you a traditionalist? Do you prefer the three-day stuff to the one-day?

ROBERT   I must admit that I am a bit of a traditionalist. I find that the one-day game is very entertaining, but it's not cricket. It's a different sort of game.

BRIAN   It's a competition. It's can you score faster than I can? I often come along for the second half of a Sunday game because someone's got to get so many runs in so many overs. How they get it is of no interest to me.

ROBERT   Exactly. I was at the Oval a couple of years ago at a Test Match and suddenly realised that I'd sat with complete attention for about an hour, during which time only about 8 or 9 runs were scored. But what was important was that there was a battle going on that was absolutely enthralling. It was not about scoring runs. It was about survival, and I loved every minute of it.

BRIAN   And the bowler trying to bowl people out, which

makes such a change. There's this awful business of just containing.

ROBERT   Yes, and all this leg stump stuff.

BRIAN   Did you ever see Godfrey Evans keep wicket?

ROBERT   Oh, yes, did I ever.

BRIAN   Did you think he was any good? I should explain that Godders has just come into the box with the latest odds from Ladbroke's.

ROBERT   He's kept to me, in fact, at one time or another.

BRIAN   Godders, what did you think of Robert Powell's bowling?

GODFREY EVANS   I thought that if he'd learnt a bit earlier he could have easily played for the county and possibly the country.

BRIAN   Which country?

GODFREY   Well, Denmark, maybe.

ROBERT   Or Madagascar.

BRIAN   Was he difficult? Did he gather pace off the pitch?

GODFREY   He entertained the crowd, which was the main thing.

BRIAN   They do enjoy seeing sixes being hit.

GODFREY   Oh, yes and he managed to hit the centre of the bat several times.

BRIAN   Robert, you come to Test Matches here, I've seen you. Do you follow cricket much, I mean going to watch it?

ROBERT   When I can, yes. The glorious thing about membership of the MCC, which is about as rare as hen's teeth these days, is that as I live nearby I can pop in literally for an hour or two and just watch a bit of cricket, and have a beer any time, which I enjoy.

BRIAN   Any theory about anything right or wrong with cricket nowadays? Have you got a bee in your bonnet about anything particularly?

ROBERT Well, yes I have. I think it's interesting that although the human being has changed physically since cricket began, the game is still played on a 22-yard-long pitch.

BRIAN So what you'd like is a longer pitch. I know who'd be on your side, that's our Cricket Correspondent, Christopher Martin-Jenkins, who's advocated a longer pitch for some time.

ROBERT I just think it may be something that needs looking at. There should be a certain amount of flexibility within the game, otherwise it is going to turn into a fast bowler's game and nothing else.

BRIAN Yes, when you think of the West Indians, all six foot seven or six foot eight of them.

ROBERT Yes, it's not so much here, but I think that out in the West Indies it becomes unfair. I mean, I don't think even the West Indians like batting there against their own bowlers.

BRIAN I haven't seen you in Australia watching cricket. Have you been to Australia?

ROBERT I've been to Australia. I've done a couple of pictures out there, but with appalling timing. I went during

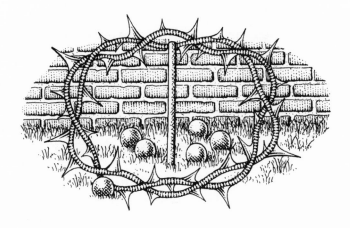

the winter, and was literally leaving Perth as the England team arrived. My agent nearly got the sack. I told him I will only do films now in Australia during the Australian summer.

BRIAN   Let's just talk a little bit about your acting.

ROBERT   Do we have to?

BRIAN   Well, we've talked about your cricket, which is very good, but then so is your acting. What was your first television role?

ROBERT   I'm glad you asked me that, as not many people know. I played 'Citizen' in episode five of *The Hunchback of Notre Dame* in 1967. I had six words which were – 'Here she comes, here she comes,' – and they cut three of them!

BRIAN   And who was she?

ROBERT   She was Esmeralda on the tumbril. There was a crowd of eighty in the studios at Ealing, and I was the only talking person in the crowd.

BRIAN   How did you do it? With a French accent?

ROBERT   No, I just said, 'Here she comes', which was probably not very French. Not very good, either. I've since worked with the director, who told me he used that scene on his lecture tours as 'how not to make television'. But he added, 'It's nothing to do with your performance, it's to do with my direction.'

BRIAN   Is there any particular actor you've admired, or copied?

ROBERT   Well, Brian Statham, I think. Maybe Dennis Lillee too . . . but as for real actors there are three, I suppose. If I had an ambition, then it was to be a combination of Peter O'Toole, Alec Guinness and Jack Lemmon.

BRIAN   What a mixture. What particular characteristic from each would you have liked?

ROBERT   The quality of O'Toole's that I admired and loved was his madness. There still is a complete unpredictability about him, which most actors aspire to, and very few can ever achieve. With Alec – and I worked with him in *King Lear* on radio – it was the ability to create a thunderstorm with a whisper.

BRIAN   He appears to act with a minimum of effort.

ROBERT   And he can do it all without making a noise about it.

I suppose I'd choose Jack Lemmon because he's one of the very few major film stars who can play ordinary people. And the very quality that you need to make you a star almost denies you that ordinariness. He's one of the most skilful actors I've seen.

BRIAN   And of the opposite sex? If I offered you a part and said, 'who would you like as your leading lady?'

ROBERT   Well, unfortunately other considerations tend to come into it, don't they? Oh, there are lots, but on the grounds that I may incriminate myself, I think I shall keep them a secret.

BRIAN   I believe it's a fact that Mrs Powell accompanies you on your various locations.

ROBERT   She used to and she still does if we're talking about school holidays. I'm taking my son on location with me soon as well. He's ten and I think it's about time he got out there.

BRIAN   Has he had some cricket coaching yet?

ROBERT   He does John Emburey's cricket camp at winter, easter and summer. He's a left arm bowler and a right hand bat, and he loves it.

BRIAN   Would you like him to be a Verity or a Voce?

ROBERT   Voce would be a nice idea.

BRIAN   We could do with someone like him. Maybe in about twelve years time – I don't think I shall be doing the commentary then – we shall be talking about Barney Powell coming in from the Pavilion End.

GARY LINEKER

AT ONE TIME IT was perfectly possible for a professional to play Test and County cricket in the summer, and International and League soccer in the winter. There are many examples of this, including Harold Makepeace, who played for Everton and England, Joe Hulme and Leslie Compton both played for Arsenal and England, Willie Watson for Huddersfield and England, and Arthur Milton for Arsenal and England. In addition, Denis Compton played for Arsenal, winning a Cup Final winners' medal, and playing in Internationals for England during the war. Patsy Hendren (Brentford), Bill Edrich (Spurs) and Brian Close (Leeds United and Arsenal) were others who played in the League but did not win an England cap. Nowadays because the two seasons overlap, it has become impossible.

In 1988 Gary was a Barcelona player, though a year later he was to join Tottenham Hotspur. He has always been a very keen cricketer, and though modest about his ability, I gather he is an excellent batsman and, as you would imagine, a fine fielder and wicket keeper too.

Gary was on the mend from a bad bout of hepatitis when he gave us this interview, but even so I was surprised to see how slight and lean he appeared. He has to take many hard knocks and withstand much ferocious tackling. But somehow he survives, and I must add, never seems to retaliate nor complain, he just gets up and gets on with it. He is undoubtedly one of the cleanest players in the game. He really seemed to enjoy his day with us in the commentary box and, for an international star of his magnitude, was unbelievably humble and friendly.

OLD TRAFFORD, 2 JULY 1988

BRIAN JOHNSTON Last year you qualified as a playing member of the MCC. How many matches did you actually play?

GARY LINEKER Well, you have to play five and I only had three weeks in England, because of living in Spain, so I had to cram a few games in. But with the MCC having games all round the country on virtually every day of the summer, it was ideal for me.

BRIAN I should explain to people that there's a waiting list of about thirty thousand for the MCC, but you can get in as a playing member if you're skilful at cricket. So this is a great tribute to your cricket. Did you write and say you wanted to play, or did somebody put you up?

GARY You have to be nominated by a couple of people, and then you have to prove your abilities as a cricketer in these five games, and also prove to be a decent sort of chap.

BRIAN   Well, you'd pass that one easily enough. What about the cricket? How many did you make last year, do you remember?

GARY   I had quite a good start at the Bank of England ground, where I got 69 or 70 or something like that. So that put me in good stead, being more of a batsman than anything else. Although I kept wicket in a few games.

BRIAN   Oh, you enjoy wicket keeping as well?

GARY   I'm a part-time wicket keeper that's all.

BRIAN   Did you have any good players playing with you?

GARY   I actually played that first game with Nick Pocock. That was nice, because I was a bit nervous for the first game. I never get nervous for football, but I was playing cricket. He settled me down.

BRIAN   Let's go back to the beginning. You're a Leicester boy?

GARY   That's right. Born and bred.

BRIAN   And you played football for Leicester, but did you play cricket as a boy there?

GARY   Yes, I played at all the representative levels until I left school at sixteen. I actually played with Russell Cobb right through school. I also played for Midland Schools, so cricket has always been a great love as well as football.

BRIAN   You had to choose between the two, did you?

GARY   Well, it wasn't really like that. I was offered an apprenticeship with Leicester City at sixteen, and it was a chance that I didn't think I could refuse. Whether I would even have been good enough at cricket I will never know, but I was certainly keen on it. I think it's difficult to say what sort of level you can achieve at that age.

BRIAN   And football clubs are apt to nab people early and offer a little bit of security in the way of money.

GARY Not a lot at that time. It was just the first opportunity that came along, and I grabbed it. I've got no regrets.

BRIAN You're only twenty-seven, might it not be possible for you to play enough cricket to make a go of it?

GARY I think you have to have extraordinary natural ability. I don't think I've got that. Obviously when I've finished playing football I shall endeavour to play as much as I can, and if I've got any ability I'll reach the highest level I can. I think you should always want to play at the highest level that you can possibly achieve.

BRIAN And one of your great assets is your speed. You're a bit of a sprinter?

GARY I'm just an all round sportsman. I think I've always had a bit of an eye for a ball, and a bit of pace. I'm a sportaholic as well. I love all sports – golf, cricket, snooker, football – you name it, I'll have a go.

BRIAN What was your best time for the hundred metres?

GARY When I was a little bit younger – I don't think I'd manage it now with all the kicks and bruises I've had – I think I ran 10.5 seconds. Natural speed has always been one of my great assets. I'm not one of the most naturally gifted footballers, like Glen Hoddle or Maradonna. I can get on the end of things in the box by using a bit of pace.

BRIAN You pounce on it rather. What's your normal weight?

GARY About twelve-and-a-half stone.

BRIAN Because inevitably you get knocked about and shoved off the ball and treated roughly. Have you had any bad injuries?

GARY I've been very very fortunate, touch wood! I just pray that it will continue. If it happens, it happens. You keep your fingers crossed, but there's no way you can stay out of trouble on the pitch thinking, I don't want to get injured. But I've just been lucky so far.

BRIAN   How long did you play for Leicester?

GARY   I was at Leicester for eight years, from starting as an apprentice to leaving.

BRIAN   And were you always in the centre forward position – can we call it centre forward nowadays?

GARY   I still call it centre forward myself. And I've always played in that position ever since I can remember playing, except the first few games I actually played for Leicester when they stuck me out on the wing. I made my debut there, replacing a great old favourite Keith Weller, and I was awful, to be quite honest. I didn't really know what I was doing.

BRIAN   You must have dashed down the wing at great pace, though.

GARY   Yes, but I was never the sort of player that can get the ball and go past a player with it. I was more likely to receive a pass behind the defence and sprint after it, so I certainly was not a natural winger.

BRIAN   Has the centre forward position changed? Do you wander more than the old centre forwards used to? I mean, Dixie Dean didn't wander much. He was up there, waiting.

GARY   I can't remember Dixie Dean! I think in the old days they used to play with two wingers, and the defenders didn't really get anything like as tight and hard and physical as they are now. So it was quite easy for the wingers to beat a man and nip a centre in for the big centre forward to nod in. There were far more goals then. It was probably more entertaining for the crowd, but football's far more physical now.

BRIAN   You have to go and get the ball a lot now, do you, you can't expect people to drop it at your feet?

GARY   It's nicer if they do. But on the Continent, if you want to get involved in the game, you do have to go and

look for the ball. The great thing is to get on the end of chances, not to worry about missing them. And if you can get to the greater percentage then the more goals you'll get.

BRIAN I know you've had an interest in snooker. How good are you?

GARY I've played at club level. I'm a great friend of Willie Thorne – he's a keen cricketer too – and of course I learned a lot from him, and got to a reasonable level without any natural ability at all.

BRIAN Would you enjoy being on the snooker circuit?

GARY To be honest, I prefer team sports. I think that snooker and golf are lonely games. I like the association of being involved with a team, like cricket or football.

BRIAN Cricket has a great asset, unlike football, in that it is a team game, but you are your own man while you're out there, and it's all up to you.

GARY I think all team games have that aspect to them, even football. If you're through and you've got the goalkeeper to beat, then it's down to you and nobody else.

I think all team games need individualism, but in the end it is the strength of the whole team that will see you through.

BRIAN   And when you were at Leicester, did you follow Leicestershire cricket? Who were your heroes?

GARY   Well, he won't thank me for this, because he's now a very good friend of mine, but David Gower was my hero. He's only a few years older than me, but I used to go down to see every game, especially in the summer holidays when I was fourteen and fifteen, and David was just starting. I think I saw his debut. I believe it was in a Sunday League game. But before that, there was Brian Davison, who I used to love to watch, who hit the ball very hard, and Ray Illingworth as well.

BRIAN   Illy was captain then.

GARY   That's right, and he brought the most successful times Leicestershire have ever had. I think it was 1975 when we won the Championship and the Benson and Hedges Cup.

BRIAN   Have you ever aspired to be a bowler then?

GARY   In my early days I bowled a few leggies, very badly. I got hit around a little bit. I used to buy a few wickets, just tossing them up.

BRIAN   Gosh, we could do with a leg-break bowler today. I should concentrate a bit on that when you retire from football if I were you. Keep batting as well and then we shall have another double-international. That would be great, wouldn't it?

GARY   I think that it's impossible now, with the length of the soccer season, to get to the level of an international cricket player. Our season lasts eleven months of the year, with training to get fit for it.

BRIAN   It's got too long, hasn't it?

GARY   It is really, especially if you're involved in the

international scene, where at the end of the season there is either a European Championship, the World Cup or a tour of God knows where. The cricket season, of course, is the same as it was. But it would be impossible to be a double-international again.

BRIAN You miss a lot of the cricket season by being in Spain.

GARY People ask me what I miss, and I can honestly say the only thing I really do miss – except for my family and friends, of course, and we see quite a bit of them – is cricket. Fortunately I can pick up the World Service and I can listen to the *Test Match Special* commentary.

BRIAN I don't suppose the Spanish evening papers have the cricket scores.

GARY No, they don't.

It is incredible how difficult it is to explain cricket in Spanish. They all say, 'Yes, we know, the one where you knock it through the hoop.' They all think it's croquet.

BRIAN Now, what about the wicket keeping?

GARY I didn't really start until I was fifteen or sixteen. I tended to get a little bit bored fielding all the time and I like to be involved, and I think one day we were struggling for a keeper and I said, 'Well, I'll give it a go.' And I enjoyed it. Obviously at first I found it a lot easier standing back, but gradually I moved up.

BRIAN It's nice standing up, isn't it?

GARY It is more fun. You need a little bit of experience though, because standing up at the wicket is the art of wicket keeping.

BRIAN And first of all you need a few spinners to get you going. Pity you can't bowl your leg-breaks to your own wicket keeping, you might stump someone off your own bowling if you did.

GARY I never got past the bat. I used to get them caught

on the boundary.

BRIAN Denis Compton always used to say that a day playing cricket was far more tiring than ninety minutes of a soccer match. Do you believe that?

GARY Yes, in a different sort of way. A long day on the legs, especially fielding, does tire you a bit. It's a different sort of thing, though. You probably get more whacks in football and when you walk off you're limping. You've got a few knocks that clear up in a day or so, whereas in cricket you have another go next day. It's a different sort of tiredness.

BRIAN How do crowds affect you? Do you find you play better in front of a big crowd, or would you be just as good playing – as some cricketers have to – in front of three men and a dog?

GARY All good professionals like to think they're as good in front of a small crowd as a big crowd, but I think it really does get the adrenalin flowing when you've got a massive crowd behind you, all cheering you on. Subconsciously or not, I do think it makes you give that little bit extra.

BRIAN You've mentioned snooker and running. Do you play golf as well?

GARY I play a little. I told you, I'll have a go at anything.

BRIAN What's your handicap?

GARY Well, living out in Spain, I'm not actually a member anywhere. But I play off about twenty. I'm an occasional sort of golfer. I used to play a lot when I was younger and then stopped playing for quite a time, and snooker took over. When I got out to Spain, I found that the weather makes golf the perfect pastime. So I've stopped playing snooker now and golf's taken over.

BRIAN Well, thank you Gary, and who knows, maybe we'll be talking to a double-international – when you give up football!

BILL PERTWEE

IT HAS ALWAYS interested me how many of the stars of variety and music hall have performed for years before receiving recognition. Arthur Askey and Tommy Trinder from seaside shows, and Sid Field and Bruce Forsyth in the provinces. With actors it is different. They can be taught and trained at drama schools or in repertory. But the only way to learn to be a comic is to go out in front of an audience and learn from bitter experience – and it can be bitter! Witness the Glasgow Empire in the old days. In the end the best are spotted by some impresario who brings them to London. Or it may be a radio show, like Arthur Askey's *Band Wagon* or Frankie Howerd's *Variety Band Box*, which turns them into stars.

A similar thing happened to Bill Pertwee, our guest at the Headingley Test Match in 1988. He had been around for a long time before his portrayal of the Chief ARP Warden Hodges in *Dad's Army* made him into a national figure in the late 1960s.

Due to rain only 23.4 overs were bowled all day on the

Saturday when Bill was with us. So we were lucky to have such a marvellous raconteur, mimic and comedian all rolled into one with us. I personally was particularly appreciative of his tales of the old seaside concert parties. When I first joined the BBC in 1946 most of my summer months in between televising the Lord's and Oval Tests (television did not reach the Midlands until 1950 and the north until 1952) were spent broadcasting from the end of piers or concert halls at the seaside resorts.

The only pity is that in a book we cannot do justice to the brilliant take-offs Bill did of his colleagues from *Dad's Army*. He also performed a number of lifelike impersonations of people like Howard Marshall, John Arlott, Raymond Glendenning, John Snagge and Frankie Howerd. Anyway his visit to us was one of the funniest due to a host of accents and voices. He was on the air for nearly an hour, because of the weather, but I'm afraid the interview has had to be considerably condensed for publication.

Before checking on his cricket, I asked him what relation he was to the playwright, Roland Pertwee.

HEADINGLEY, 23 JULY 1988

BILL PERTWEE Roland and my father were first cousins. And Roland had two sons, Jon and Michael.

BRIAN JOHNSTON Jon we all know, the famous actor; Michael people may not know so much, a great writer of films and farce and things like that. Was your side of the family theatrical?

BILL   Nothing to do with it at all. They were a farming fraternity and marine engineers in Essex, and my father went into that side of the business and then went over to Rio after the First World War. He met my mother there and married her – she was Brazilian – and then came back.

BRIAN   So what was your first job?

BILL   I started farming. We'd been evacuated down into Sussex, to a little place called Storrington. I wasn't very good at school and I wanted to leave as soon as possible, which I did when I was fifteen, and got a job as a farmer's boy, doing virtually everything. From there we had to move on so we went to stay with an aunt in Southend, and I got a job with the Southend Air and Motor Company who usually repaired the dodgem cars. But at that time they were making parts for Spitfire fighters, and if you got on the night shift the foreman said, 'We can make ourselves a few extra bob, because we're making lighters on the night shift.' He sold them for four bob, and we got something like sixpence for each.

BRIAN   So your cricket love – Sussex or Essex?

BILL   Well, really Essex – that's where it started.

BRIAN   So as a boy who was your particular hero in Essex?

BILL   I had, as a very small boy, seen Ken Farnes play.

BRIAN   What a marvellous fast bowler. I was lucky enough to see him too.

BILL   And then I got to know several of the Essex players, because I was starting to play cricket there. In fact when I was in that engineering firm at Southend – this was 1946 – I was playing a lot of club cricket. A lot of people still hadn't been demobbed, and the clubs wanted to get going, so we all got a chance and several of us had a trial for Essex.

BRIAN   What were you?

BILL   I went in about number five and was a first change

bowler, I seamed it a wee bit. The most amazing thing was that I was in the nets one night and a tall gentleman came up to me. He said, 'I understand you might want to make cricket your career.' So I said, 'Well, I'm just enjoying it at the moment.' And he said, 'I think the best thing for me to do is to get you a job in my office and then you can play as much cricket as you like.' 'But I've got a job.' He said, 'No, no, I mean a job where you won't have to do anything. You can play cricket as much as you like and still get paid.' He was a chap called F.P. Knox of Oxley Knox and Company, stockjobbers. He said, 'Come and see me on Monday week.' So I said, 'All right, thank you very much.' Naturally, I took the job as I was then able to play weekday cricket, weekend cricket, anything I liked.

A little while after that I was playing at Shoeburyness against the British Empire Eleven, which was then captained by C.B. Clarke, and T.N. Pearce the Essex captain was there and he said, 'I understand you might be thinking of taking cricket seriously.' I said, 'Well, it would be quite nice.' He said, 'Don't do it. You have no patience, you want to hit the cover off the ball every time.' So I said, 'Yes, I do enjoy it.' He said, 'I've been watching you. Oh, sure, you might get 40 or 50 or something, but a lot of the time you're not going to get anything at all. You've got to get right to the very top to make money in cricket. Have you got any means outside cricket?' I said, 'Not a ha'penny.' 'Then don't do it,' he said.

BRIAN   Now, looking back, do you think that was good advice?

BILL   Yes, very good.

BRIAN   Because you wouldn't have made it, do you think?

BILL   No, definitely not. It didn't really matter to me, because I was enjoying it anyway.

BRIAN   So you've played cricket all your life then, and

you still play for the Taverners?

BILL Yes, I do just occasionally. When the knees stand up to it.

BRIAN But it's great fun isn't it, the Taverners, playing with ex-Test cricketers?

BILL I play maybe three or four times a summer now. One of the great bonuses of being in the theatre is that you get to meet all the cricketing fraternity, and it is a wonderful bonus.

BRIAN Like other actors then, you do have time to watch cricket. Any special heroes and people you've picked out?

BILL Well, I suppose, because I got to know them socially, my heroes were Denis Compton and Bill Edrich, who were lovely people to be with. And last year I was up in Sheffield at a dinner and Sir Len Hutton was there and he said, 'We don't live far from one another, you must come over and have coffee.' And I went over one morning. Now that was wonderful, because I remember listening with my father in 1938 to his record innings described by Howard Marshall. Those are wonderful things.

I also played a match with Learie Constantine once, when I was at Southend, and many, many years later I was on the underground in London and he was sitting opposite

me and I thought, 'He won't remember, of course he won't.' And he suddenly leaned over and tapped me on the knee and said, 'We played cricket together, didn't we?'

BRIAN That's rather nice. So cricket's obviously been a great love of your life. When did the acting start?

BILL When I realised that cricket was not going to be my career, I looked through the newspapers and found an advert for Burberry's in the Haymarket wanting some-body to join their sports department, which was just opening. So in I go. At that time everything was rationed, and so you got to know lots of people who were pressing pound notes into your hand. In between, though, I had a wonderful session with the Indian cricketers in 1946.

BRIAN This was as baggage master. How did that come about?

BILL I got an introduction to Vijay Merchant and he and the team were staying at the Berners Hotel. So I went up there. I got buttonholed by Mushtaq Ali, who said – and I don't know why – 'We want clothing coupons. A lot of clothing coupons.' So I said, 'Yes, I might be able to get some.' And I thought, 'this is a way in, here.' So then I was getting clothing coupons all over the place for Mankad and Amarnath and the rest.

BRIAN You'd better be careful. You can still be prose-cuted for that.

BILL One night soon afterwards I went to the Berners Hotel and I said, 'Mr Mushtaq Ali, please.' And just behind me was another fellow who said, 'Oh, I'd like to see him as well.' They said, 'What's the name?' So I said, 'Tell him it's Bill. I've got some news for him.' And the fellow behind said, 'Detective Inspective Spooner of Bow Street.' So I shot off into the toilet as quick as possible and locked myself in there. I thought, 'I'm part of this. They've copped him. I'm going to be in the nick as well.' I was in there perspiring, when all of a sudden the door opened and Mushtaq said, 'Where are you, Billy? Come out, silly boy, come out. What are you doing in there?' I said, 'There's a policeman out there.' 'He's a great friend of mine. He's coming to see one of the matches. Come out. You've got all the coupons for me?' And then he said, 'You must come round with us.' And I thought, 'Well, I'm not doing anything. Why not?' And I had a bit of time with them.

BRIAN Someone you must have met then was John Arlott, who went round with them. That was his first commentary job.

BILL Yes, I did meet John. And at that time something I really wanted to do was commentate. But I didn't ask John, I'd only met him very briefly, though he was very polite. But I phoned him up at the ground and he said, 'Go and see Angus McKay of *Sports Report*.'

So I did, and I got a Chelsea match to do and he said, 'It won't be on the air, but it's just to see how you go. You'd better get a cab back.' So I got in this cab, got into a traffic jam, and arrived back something like an hour late.

BRIAN By which time the programme was off the air?

BILL Oh, long gone. And he looked at what I'd written and I said, 'It's not very good, is it? I was nervous that I wouldn't get back and I was writing the notes in the cab.' It was just a ludicrous thought that I might have a future as a sports writer.

BRIAN So that came to nowt. So far we haven't heard about a single step on the boards. When did you get into acting and how?

BILL Burberry's closed their sports department, it wasn't really their cup of tea. But one of my customers who I'd got to know very well, said, 'I've got a thriving office and window-cleaning business and it's really taking off. How much do you make here?' I told him I got six pounds a week, plus one per cent commission. He offered more and so I went, and I was window cleaning.

BRIAN What, up the ladder?

BILL Yes, I was up a ladder or in those cradles.

BRIAN Was George Formby right? Did you see things when you were cleaning windows?

BILL Well, there were one or two things. I got involved in one in Bryanston Square, I remember. But I won't . . .

BRIAN Oh, won't you?

So you still weren't on the boards.

BILL In 1954 I had a few days' leave and my cousin, Jon Pertwee, who I'd only recently met said, 'I'm going on a variety tour. Do you want to come out with me and have a bit of fun? I'm taking a caravan. You can help me if you want. If not, you can use it as a bit of a holiday.' So I got involved with him a little bit, doing some props and mending one or two things. We met Beryl Reid about the second week, and she said that she was going into London for eight weeks to do a revue, which was a try-out for material for a television series. She said, 'I'm looking for material.' And talk about fools rush in, I said, 'I can write you some funny lines.'

BRIAN Had you written before?

BILL No, of course I hadn't. But I wrote a couple of pieces and she said, 'We'll have them both.' One of them was about a village cricket match and the other one was about a weather forecast.

Well, about three days before the revue was due to open, the producer rang me and said, 'Somebody has dropped out at the last minute, but you know the material, could you do it?' So I said, 'Well, I'm window cleaning. I get up at five o'clock, but I do finish at half past three.' You didn't have to worry about Equity cards or

anything like that. It was at the Watergate Theatre Club, just off the Strand, so I went there. Barry Sinclair was in the revue and a fellow called Dougie Argent, who later became a BBC director. And I was in the dressing room, whistling. Well, Barry got hold of me and threw me out of the dressing room. He said, 'Go outside. Turn round three times.'

BRIAN It's an old superstition. You musn't whistle in a dressing room, must you?

BILL I thought, 'there are some lunatics here.' I finished after the eight weeks and that was the end of it. Back to the window cleaning, and I was making the money there. But after a few months I thought, 'I'm bored with this. I'd like to do some more on the stage.'

BRIAN The call of the greasepaint.

BILL So I phoned my cousin up and he said, 'It's such a precarious business, you're mad. If you do you've got to start at the bottom. Go to the agents and see if you can get a job in a rep or a concert party somewhere.'

The first bloke I went to said, 'Yes, I've got a concert party going off to Gorleston near Yarmouth. The governor needs somebody cheap.' So I said, 'What's cheap?' He said, 'Nine pounds a week.' I said, 'Oh no, I've been earning much more than that. I couldn't possibly do it under ten pounds.' Anyway he rang me later and said, 'All right, they'll do ten pounds.' Now, I didn't know that I had to do five ten-minute solo spots.

BRIAN   Then you had to write some material.

BILL   Now I was in trouble. I had terrible sleepless nights and I fell back on impressions. I was pretty terrible and in fact one of the ladies in the show went to the governor after the first few weeks and said, 'He has got to go. He is an amateur.' And the governor said, 'He works cheap. He's not going.' And the lady who had asked for me to go is now my wife.

Then from those concert parties you got into a bigger show and then a bigger show and then the radio came along. *Beyond our Ken* and *Round the Horne*. But before that I was a comic at the Windmill. And that was very difficult, because they didn't come in to see the comics.

BRIAN   Were there really dirty old men in macs who used to climb over the seats to get into the front row?

BILL   Oh, yes. On a Saturday we used to have farmers up from Somerset and they used to bring their sandwiches, and as soon as the comics came on they'd open their sandwiches and they'd be passing them round.

BRIAN   If someone in the front row got up to leave there was a scramble.

BILL   Oh, the noise! Up went the seats behind – bang!

BRIAN   Did Vivian Van Damm mind if you didn't get laughs?

BILL   He didn't mind. He used to say, 'You'll get so bored with not getting laughs, you'll think of something original.' And that is what happened.

BRIAN   I don't know if we're ever going to get on to *Dad's Army*. Who spotted you for that? Was it the radio work that got you into the BBC?

BILL   Yes. It was. It also taught me how to read, because if you worked with Kenneth Horne, Kenneth Williams,

Hugh Paddick and Betty Marsden with only two hours' rehearsal, maybe less, you'd got to be able to read a script. And that helped me with the television. I was with *Beyond our Ken* from 1959 to 1968, and when that finished I got a letter from David Croft asking me to phone him. And he said, 'We're doing the pilot of a show. It was going to be called *The FightingTigers*, but it's now *Dad's Army*. There's a couple of lines in it for you, as an air raid warden.' I'd worked with David on a *Hugh and I* in which I had a couple of lines. And he said, 'You looked a bit of a bombast and a bit of a bully in that, so I thought you'd be all right.' I think they needed a private Hitler for Arthur Lowe. They couldn't have a general, because the general would naturally win. They had to have somebody who would be a bombast, but would lose.

BRIAN   And you put on this marvellous bombastic thing. You must have had tremendous fun.

BILL   Yes. It was. It became a great big family. We did eighty-seven episodes for tv, plus specials and a film, a stage show of it and sixty radio broadcasts. They had originally wanted John Le Mesurier to be the officer and Arthur Lowe to be the sergeant, because that's exactly what they had been in the war. Arthur was a sergeant major in the middle east and John was a captain, I think. They decided to reverse it so that there would always be aggro between the two.

BRIAN   It's become a piece of history in BBC Television. Where was it done?

BILL   The hall was a studio. All the other stuff was done round Thetford. They were marvellous days, and we had David Croft weather. There was only one day in nine years when we couldn't film. It was beautifully cast and the writing was good. They wrote situations, they didn't write jokes. The jokes came out of the situations.

DAVID ESSEX

I HAD SEEN HIM IN *Godspell* and *Evita*, had enjoyed his tv series *The River*, and had listened to and liked his records. I also knew that he was a passionate lover of cricket who played for Tim Rice's Heartaches and Eric Clapton's XI. But I had never met him. So I was delighted when David Essex agreed to come to the second Test at Lord's in 1989. It was at some inconvenience to himself, as he was going off that day on a family holiday in the South of France.

He was, as I suspected, quietly spoken with expressive eyes and a friendly smile. He still looked remarkably young though he admitted to being 'fortyish'. What was quite obvious from the moment he entered the box, was his great interest and love of cricket. He watched every ball and was clearly thrilled to be at a Lord's Test Match. He has passed on his love of the game to his twelve-year-old son, Danny, of whom he has high hopes as a future England cricketer.

I was a bit naughty as we came to the end of our time. But I just couldn't resist it. In 1951 I had sung *Underneath the Arches* with Bud Flanagan in my 'live' spot on *In Town Tonight*. By arrangement with him I wheeled a street piano up to the stage door of the Victoria Palace where the Crazy Gang were performing. At a signal Bud came out, put his hand on my shoulder, and we sang the song together. I didn't let on to Bud that it was the only tune I could play on the piano. So on this lovely sunny day at Lord's I thought I would invite David to follow Bud and sing it with me. I hadn't warned him, and we hadn't rehearsed, so perhaps it's just as well that you cannot hear the result. As we came to the last two lines he whispered to me, 'Come on, build it up to a big finish.' We did so, and at least he and I thought we were good! But I am going to be immodest. It was chosen for *Pick of the Week* the following Friday, and on New Year's Eve 1989 it was repeated on *Pick of the Year*! I'm glad that someone else enjoyed it as well as us.

I was longing to find out about his cricket, but before I did so I had to ask him about the single earring which he was wearing.

LORD'S, 24 JUNE 1989

BRIAN JOHNSTON   Before we move on to cricket, I once interviewed a chap on *Down Your Way* who, like you, had one earring and I said, 'What an extraordinary thing to have one earring,' and he said, 'I'd look an awful fool with two.' Would you look an awful fool with two?

DAVID ESSEX   I think so, yes. I have it because on my

mother's side there's a kind of gypsy background, and it was put into my ear at a very early age by a relative and it caused a few problems at school.

BRIAN   And is that the same one you've always had?

DAVID   No, I tend to lose them. I take them out when I wash my hair and they disappear.

BRIAN   Let's talk about your cricket. I hear glowing reports of you from Tim Rice. You play for his Heartaches team, don't you?

DAVID   Well yes, but he's obviously a liar. I am a lousy cricketer. I am a lousy all-rounder. I enjoy cricket very much. I play some club cricket and I play for Tim, as you said, and I also play for the Eric Clapton XI. In fact we played most of the Australian team on Monday and we won. It was at Northampton for charity. They were terrific, because they'd played all day against Northants, and at six o'clock we had a match for a children's charity.

BRIAN   And how did D. Essex fare?

DAVID   I did all right. I came in to bowl to Steve Waugh and I bowled what I thought was a pretty excellent ball, yorker length, bit of movement in the air and of course it went for six, which I thought was a bit much. But my fondest memory is that my son, Danny, who's twelve, played and Dennis Waterman was at the other end and Danny came in for the last over and they put Merv Hughes on to bowl.

BRIAN   Had he got a helmet on?

DAVID   No helmet, big pads. Seven slips they set. Merv Hughes came running in from the sight screen. Danny lifted his bat. Merv floated down this lovely ball and Danny hit it for four. The crowd went nuts. Merv waved his fist. It was really lovely.

BRIAN   Any chance of seeing Danny Essex playing for Essex or England?

DAVID   Well, he's very keen. He loves the game and the main thing is he enjoys it. I don't know how much ability he will eventually have. Only time will tell. But he does love it and I love it, too.

BRIAN   What sort of pace have you got when you bowl?

DAVID   It's medium club class, which is very slow at Test level.

BRIAN   Do you have to bat high up the order, because you're always going off to some concert?

DAVID   Well, I like to say that. That's my excuse, because I can't stand going in at ten and trying to bash around for runs. I like to go in around four or five really. But the batting's come on because I started really as a bowler.

The story of me and cricket is quite strange really, because I captained the school cricket team – but it was never a passion – football was always the passion. Cricket really only came about because of my son, Danny. A couple of years ago he kept saying, 'Dad, come and bowl at me.' So he brought me back into the game. And for the last two years I really could have been a professional amateur cricketer, I've been playing more or less every day in all these teams that I moonlight in. It's great fun.

BRIAN   I think I read somewhere that you failed deliberately in your exams so that you could go to a school that played soccer rather than rugger. Is that right? You would have had to play rugby in a grammar school.

DAVID   Yes, I drew Popeye on the exam paper.

BRIAN   How many marks did they give you for that?

DAVID   The drawing wasn't very good, so I don't think I got many marks for it. It was a maths exam.

BRIAN   Where did you go to school, then?

DAVID   In east London. They've pulled the school down now. It was a lousy school. It was the kind of school that had a terrible reputation and therefore attracted not quite good enough teachers. It was like a vicious circle. The sport was good. The football was very good and we played cricket, which was something. It was a state school.

BRIAN   Was it organised cricket, or just rough stuff?

DAVID   There wasn't any coaching. We played on matting on an asphalt base.

BRIAN   You must have got the ball to move a bit there.

DAVID   Well, it was a sort of big pudding ball. If you could get it to the next wicket it was an achievement.

BRIAN   So you were born in the East End?

DAVID   Yes, I was born in Plaistow.

BRIAN   And Essex is an assumed name.

DAVID   Yes. The trouble was, that when I wanted to join Equity there was an actor called David Cook, which is my real name, and you cannot join the union with the same name as an existing member. I was living in Essex and it seemed a pleasant name. I'm glad it wasn't Middlesex.

BRIAN   That might have been taken wrong I think. So when did you begin to take an interest in music?

DAVID   Well, I used to go on adventures into Soho from about the age of thirteen. The East End was great. It was a great playground, because it was bombed a lot in the Second World War, and that left us kids with lots of bomb craters and air raid shelters and bits of houses to run in and out of. So it was lovely. But to catch the bus up to the West End where all the music and the clubs and the bright lights were, that was real adventure. And I was strolling along Wardour Street one day and I just heard some music coming out of a basement, and I went down with a friend of mine, who I think became a milkman, and I was besotted by the music. I was thirteen and I just knew I had to be a musician.

BRIAN   Would it have been my sort of music?

DAVID   Yes, though it wasn't Flanagan and Allen.

BRIAN   Well, I'm Novello more, you see.

DAVID   Then it wouldn't have been. This was R and B music, which is short for rhythm and blues.

BRIAN   That's all right, I like that, too. So then did you try and learn an instrument?

DAVID   Well, it seemed to me, because I didn't have a lot of patience – I've got more now – that if you hit a drum it answered immediately back. So it seemed sensible to learn the drums. Later I played guitar very badly, and I write on the keyboards. So I've branched out since the drums, but they were the first thing.

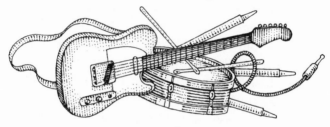

BRIAN   When did the voice come?

DAVID   That was all fluke and luck really, because all I ever wanted to be was a jazz drummer. Now all I want to be is a professional cricketer, but at that time I just wanted to be a jazz drummer. And I was playing the drums and the lead guitarist turned round one day and said, 'Look, man, I can't play lead guitar and sing at the same time, so someone else has got to sing,' and they all pointed at me. So I started singing these strange urban Chicago blues songs and that was it. It went downhill from there, Brian.

BRIAN   You've got a very recognisable voice. It's quite different from anyone else's. Did you have any lessons?

DAVID   Not really, no. I did a lot of work in repertory, and so I was able to make major mistakes in front of small audiences so it didn't matter too much.

BRIAN   So you did some straight acting?

DAVID   Yes, I've played Byron for the Young Vic.

BRIAN   Did he win?

DAVID   No, he definitely lost. It was very interesting, but I always feel like a musician that acts rather than an actor who sings.

BRIAN   I first saw you in *Godspell*.

DAVID   That was a marvellous show.

BRIAN   I thought it was and I remember you were carried out through the auditorium.

DAVID   The strange thing about *Godspell* was that we rehearsed and rehearsed and the theatre that we were supposed to open in suddenly cancelled. They'd seen ten hippies running around and they thought, no, this is rubbish. So the only place that we could open was at the Roundhouse. And it opened, and there were queues round the block. It was phenomenal. It was a terrific cast with Jeremy Irons as John the Baptist, and Marti Webb and Julie Covington, and although I was playing Jesus, there wasn't really a star. It was very much an ensemble type of show.

BRIAN   It preceded *Jesus Christ Superstar*, didn't it? I don't know if that gave them the idea.

DAVID   I don't know, sometimes these things are in the air. Ideas seem to come at the same time. It was a very different show.

BRIAN   Was *Godspell* a moving thing to play?

DAVID   It was, yes. I used to hear people crying and sobbing. It was something special. I did it for two years and the strangest thing was the interval, where the audience would come up and have a glass of wine.

BRIAN   That's right, it was all very friendly, but it didn't give you much rest in the interval did it?

DAVID   What was extraordinary was people's reaction to me playing Jesus. They really were awestruck. So you felt you had this tremendous responsibility for people's innermost faith. It was a great show. It's probably the show I've enjoyed most.

BRIAN   And two years. Do you mind the routine of a long run?

DAVID   I do actually, yes. The incredible thing is that, although the monotony of the routine does get you down and change your life, really, every night is different and the inter-relationship between the actors and audience is always different. So that gives you a stimulus.

BRIAN   Did you enjoy doing *Evita*?

DAVID   I did. The great thing about *Evita* was that it was under an intense spotlight. Everyone was very interested in the show, it was very difficult to get tickets, and it was a big success. But the overriding thing for me was that I was able to do it for just six months, which was brilliant.

BRIAN   What was that thing you sang at the start?

DAVID   'Oh, What a Circus'.

BRIAN   What about the Tim Rice lyrics. He's your captain in the Heartaches, so you'd better be careful.

DAVID   Oh, what a marvellous cricketer.

BRIAN   I asked about his lyrics! I know he's a great slow left-arm bowler.

DAVID   I think Tim's lyrics are very good. I think one of the songs in *Evita*, 'High Flying Adored', is probably one of the finest popular lyrics written in the last thirty years. He has this knack of directness and of using unusual words in a direct context.

BRIAN   So when did you start composing? You've had two number one hits in this country, haven't you?

DAVID   Yes and twenty-three top thirties.

BRIAN   Not bad.

DAVID   The writing came about because it just seemed more honest to sing things that had come from you, you know, lyrically and musically.

BRIAN   You're a clever boy, but how do you sit down and write a tune?

DAVID   I sit down using keyboards, mainly the piano, but it's a strange process. I've got a new album out called *Touching the Ghost* and the title song outlines how intangible songwriting is, and how difficult it is to tell where the creative spark comes from.

BRIAN   Where do you get your spark? In the bath, or walking about, or in the middle of a big innings?

DAVID   Never in the middle of a big innings. I once made up a song in Antigua during a session in the outfield spent waiting for another West Indian to hit a big six. It's called, 'Look at the Sun', because I was looking into the sun and I thought, 'Well, all these balls are just going over my head. I'll make a song up.' That's the only one.

   Generally I think I store pictures and images. I'm very much an observer. As an only child, I think you spend more time by yourself. So I watch and store things, and then when the commitment is there to write I'll sit at the piano and do it. But I only really write out of panic, 'We're in the studio on Monday, have you written the songs?' sort of thing.

BRIAN   What do you think is your public? Is it basically young people, or are you amongst the oldies as well?

DAVID   I think it's a fair mixture now, because I've been at it a fair while.

BRIAN   Now, I did sing 'Underneath the Arches' with Bud Flanagan. It would give me great pleasure to sing it with you. Do you know the words?

DAVID   I don't, really. We'll kind of wing it. Are you Ches or Bud?

BRIAN   I'm Bud really. You can do the Ches thing.
(And they did. Ed.)